Make me a channel

Make me a channel

ROY LAWRENCE

SCRIPTURE UNION

Scripture Union, 207–209 Queensway, Bletchley MK2 2EB, England.

© Roy Lawrence 1996

First published 1996

ISBN 1 85999 015 0

British Library Cataloguing-in-Publication Data
A catalogue record for this book is available from the British Library.

Unless otherwise attributed, scripture quotations are taken from the HOLY BIBLE, NEW INTERNATIONAL VERSION. Copyright © 1973, 1978, 1984 by International Bible Society. Anglicisation copyright © 1979, 1984, 1989. Used by permission of Hodder and Stoughton Limited.

Extracts from The Book of Common Prayer, the rights in which are vested in the Crown, are reproduced by permission of the Crown's Patentee, Cambridge University Press.

Cover illustration by Janice Nicolson.
Cover design by Mark Carpenter Design Consultants.

Printed and bound in Great Britain by Cox & Wyman Ltd, Reading.

This book is gratefully dedicated to my wife, Eira,
without whose loving input
my own output would have been
a mere fraction of itself

Make me a channel of your peace.
Where there is hatred let me bring your love;
Where there is injury, your pardon, Lord;
And where there's doubt, true faith in you.

Sebastian Temple
An adaptation of words attributed to St Francis of Assisi
Copyright © Franciscan Communications 1967

CONTENTS

1 The input/output people 9

2 Receiving forgiveness – Channelling forgiveness 15

3 Receiving kindness – Channelling kindness 25

4 Receiving God's love – Channelling God's love 33

5 Receiving healing – Channelling healing 41

6 Receiving truth – Channelling truth 49

7 Receiving freedom – Channelling freedom 57

8 Receiving hope – Channelling hope 63

9 Receiving faith – Channelling faith 71

10 Receiving joy – Channelling joy 79

11 Receiving the world's goods – Channelling the world's goods 85

12 *Warning!* Receiving evil influences – Channelling evil influences 93

13 Onward, Christian soldiers 101

14 Receiving Jesus – Channelling Jesus 109

15 Receiving eternal life – Channelling eternal life 115

Epilogue – This is your life 123

The stories in this book are all based on real events; but in order to preserve anonymity, most of the names and a few of the details have been changed.

Chapter 1

THE INPUT/OUTPUT PEOPLE

The Bible makes extraordinary claims about the experience of being a Christian. St Paul writes: '[When anyone is joined to Christ] he becomes a new person altogether – the past is finished and gone, everything has become fresh and new' (2 Corinthians 5:17, *J B Phillips*). Jesus promises: 'I have come to bring [you] life in all its fullness' (John 10:10, *J B Phillips*).

So why is this a million miles away from what many Christians actually feel as they try to live out their faith?

Susanna's husband was a prominent leader in a prosperous church nearby. She came to see me because she felt a total failure as a Christian. 'In our church,' she said, 'we are supposed to live victorious and glowing Christian lives. But I just don't feel victorious. I feel ill and depressed and angry and ashamed. I'm letting my husband and my church down. I'm probably letting God down too. I'm a failure.'

She was very surprised when the first thing I did was to congratulate her. In fact, she had taken the first essential step towards becoming an effective, liberated person. She had been *honest*. Honesty will always be necessary if we are to become effective and liberated Christians – that honesty which can sometimes provoke us to laugh at ourselves and sometimes bring us to tears.

St Paul had this kind of honesty. Although he believed Jesus creates new persons out of old sinners, he knew that Jesus does not do this by waving a magic wand: he does it on the basis of partnership. This is not an equal partnership. On his part, Jesus is totally committed to us and to his relationship with us: his death on a cross proves it. By contrast, we are far from totally committed: we are weak, wobbly and wayward on our side of the partnership. We may sing, 'Onward Christian soldiers' with great gusto, but often what we manage is more like a samba than a march – one step forward, one step back.

St Paul writes: 'What I do is not the good I want to do; no, the evil I do not want to do – this I keep on doing … in my inner being I delight in God's law; but I see another law at work in the members of my body … What a wretched man I am! Who will rescue me from the body of death?' (Romans 7:19–24).

Fortunately, he knows the answer: 'Thanks be to God [who does this] through Jesus Christ our Lord' (Romans 7:25). We can know it too, but to do so we have first to recognise a fundamental principle of life. This principle is so basic that you can see it at work in ordinary household gadgets.

My wife and I have a radio by the side of our bed. When we get up in the morning, we listen to the news and current affairs on BBC Radio 4 or on local Radio. Occasionally, if we find ourselves awake in the middle of the night, we switch on the World Service and find it often sends us off to sleep again! On my day off I spend some of my free time enjoying the music on Classic FM or Radio 3.

If we had to do without our radio, we really would miss it. But, of course, it would not be any use to us unless two things were true: the station we want must be broadcasting, and we must have switched on and tuned in the radio. In other words, there has to be *input* and *output* before the radio will work. In the middle of the night we could twiddle the knobs on the set to our hearts' content, but we would not receive Radio 4 because Radio 4 does not broadcast at night. And on my day off the airwaves could be resonating with the glories of Bach, Beethoven and Brahms, but these would fail to reach me if I had not switched my radio on.

As I write, the weather outside is horrible: rain, sleet and snow have been bucketing down all morning. However, in my study it is snug and warm because our central heating system is on. Once again the input/output principle is in operation. The North West Water Board provides the water; British Gas enables the boiler to provide the heat; the radiators in the study are switched on. Everything is working well. It was different a couple of years ago when the water pipes froze and the input was interrupted. It is different in our spare bedroom where the radiator is switched off, and so the output is interrupted.

The input/output principle is obvious in terms of household gadgets, but it is equally true of people and it is absolutely fundamental in understanding Christianity. If we want to be effective and liberated, we must first be honest – as honest as Susanna or St Paul. But we need not linger in the pain that honesty inevitably brings. We need to go back to basics, back to the Bible, back to the Lord of the Bible, back to his own input/output principle. Consider these words of Jesus:

Output 'A new command I give you: Love one another…'
Input   'As I have loved you…' *(John 13:34)*

Output 'If you hold to my teaching, you are really my
          disciples…'
Input   'Then you will know the truth and the truth will
          set you free.' *(John 8:31–32)*
Input   'Freely you have received …'
Output '… freely give.' *(Matthew 10:8)*

Over the centuries, there has been a tendency in the church
for many of its members to listen to only half of Jesus'
teaching about input and output. Some have put all the
stress on output. A group known as the Pelagians were very
hot on good deeds – that is, on *output.* They thought that if
you performed enough of them, you could work your ticket
to heaven. But they were weak on input. They failed to see
that we can't pull ourselves up by our own bootlaces. Good
deeds have to be enabled. The gospel is a gift, not a
requirement.

On the other hand, others put all the stress on *input.* A
group known as the Antinomians (Greek for 'those who are
against the law') knew all about the gospel being a gift
from God, his input into us. But they were distinctly cool
about output. They taught that receiving the saving love of
Jesus need not make any difference to the way you live.
You could celebrate being saved by deliberately going on
sinning!

The church had the wisdom to recognise that both groups
were talking nonsense.

All this happened in the early centuries of church history,
but many Christians today need to learn the lesson that was
learned then. The Pelagian heresy goes down particularly
well with the traditional British stiff upper lip. But beware
– without proper input we may end up as guilt-ridden neu-
rotics, endlessly chasing an unachievable target and getting
nearer a workaholic breakdown day by day.

However, for others in our permissive society Antinomianism can have an appeal. Once again we need to beware, because without output we can degenerate into loveless, hypocritical slogan-slingers, all mouth and no muscle, all theory and no reality. And now, back to the Bible...

Input   'How great is the love the Father has lavished on us, that we should be called children of God! And that is what we are! ... This is how we know what love is: Jesus Christ laid down his life for us...'

Output   'And we ought to lay down our lives for our brothers ... let us not love with words or tongue but with actions and in truth.' *(1 John 3:1–18)*

Bishop Frank Sargeant has composed a memorable little prayer: 'Lord make me a channel, not a bucket!' The great thing about a channel is that it has both input *and* output. And Jesus invites his followers to be 'input/output' people. This should be one of the prime principles behind Christian living.

But how does it work in practice?

Chapter 2

RECEIVING FORGIVENESS

CHANNELLING FORGIVENESS

If someone were to ask me to make a list of the basic needs of the human spirit, I could make a good case for putting our need for forgiveness at the top. Certainly the entrance to the Christian church is through a door marked 'Forgiveness' – and there is no other door.

We do not find this an easy or comfortable thought, but it is a basic Christian conviction that we human beings are sinners. We are breakers of God's laws, all of us. (If you turn to chapter six, you will find some of the evidence for this sweeping statement.) If this seems like bad news, there is worse to come: the sin that is part of us all puts us at deep risk, making the human race an endangered species both globally and individually.

Globally, it is possible, as never before, for humankind to bring the world as we know it to an end. We have the power of nuclear overkill – the wrong finger on the wrong button could trigger a massive nuclear explosion followed by counter-attacks and chain reactions – and we have enough nuclear weapons to destroy the world many times over. Or the explosion could be a self-induced breakout of disease – AIDS or something worse. Or the disaster could be ecological, such as irreparable damage to the ozone layer, which would in turn do irreparable damage to us. Our sins seem to have the power to make us stupid – stupid enough to destroy the very things we depend on for life. It is an undeniable fact that we are cherishing neither our planet nor our universe. It should come as no surprise, therefore, when they strike back at us.

If we are in danger at a global level, we are in no less danger as individual human souls. The Bible tells us that God means us to discover joy on earth and even greater joy in eternity. However, breaking God's law prevents this discovery. It is bad enough that sin spoils our relationships with the people around us; it is bad enough that it gives us completely the wrong attitude to our own inner self. But the worst consequence of our sin is that it cuts us off from our Creator, blocking our chances of knowing him now and cutting us off from the eternal life which is God's plan for us. Sin turns us into hell-raisers in terms of this life and hell-bent in terms of the next. The Bible puts it starkly: 'All have sinned and fall short of the glory of God' (Romans 3:23). 'The wages of sin is death' (Romans 6:23).

Against this background of crisis, the Christian faith brings the gospel – the 'good news'. God is on our side. He has no wish to see us self-destruct, and he has a secret weapon to bring against our self-destructive tendencies: that weapon is his forgiveness. We enter the presence of God through a door marked 'Forgiveness', and Jesus Christ is that door (John 10:9).

There is nothing sloppy or shallow or sentimental about this. For Jesus to be our door of forgiveness, he had to leave the glories of heaven and come into our world to show us what God is like and how human life should be; but he also had to die on the cross. In a line from that famous hymn 'There is a green hill' – 'He died that we might be forgiven'. This is an amazing concept, too great for our small minds. To receive 'through his blood, the forgiveness of sins' (Ephesians 1:7) is a mystery we can barely begin to comprehend.

Perhaps the world of human relationships affords us some help as we try to understand the meaning of the cross. Jesus said, 'Greater love has no-one than this, that he lay down his life for his friends' (John 15:13). I have had the privilege of meeting several people who found that loving and forgiving have brought them close to sharing in this greater love.

Lydia lived in one of my former parishes. Her husband used to knock her about and was unashamedly unfaithful to her. When I asked her how she could stand it, she said, 'Well, there really is a better side to him and I think I may be his only hope of becoming the man he could be.' So she stayed with him and went on offering him love and forgiveness. Her bruises showed the price that she paid. She reminded me of Nancy from Charles Dickens' *Oliver Twist*. In *Oliver!* – the musical show based on Charles Dickens' novel, currently enjoying a successful revival at the London Palladium – Nancy sings that she must go on loving and forgiving Bill Sykes 'as long as he needs me'. But she finds that the cost of that love and forgiveness is her life.

Eleanor's son became a drug addict, and for five years he bullied her and stole from her. She did not condone either the drug-taking or the conduct that went with it. When I visited her, I could see the pain etched on her face. Yet she could not and did not stop caring. 'You've got to forgive,' she said. Good mothers are like that.

And good husbands and fathers are like that too. Bernard had to undergo the pain of watching his wife, Ethel, die slowly of cancer. Perhaps the worst thing about her illness was that the cancer affected Ethel's mind causing her to turn against her husband. Day by day she heaped abuse on Bernard. His response was patient love and unfailing care right up to the moment of her death. Personally, I have no doubt that Ethel is not only singing the Lord's praises in heaven now, but her husband's praises too! Bernard would be most embarrassed if I were to tell him that I could see God in him, but again and again he reminded me of the way in which God loves and forgives – and pays the price of doing so.

Whatever horrors the human race perpetrates, however we fail to love him and to love each other, God has never stopped caring. He 'has to forgive' because that is his nature. In Jesus Christ, God has come among us, not to condone our sins but to offer us that costly forgiveness which alone can draw us back to himself. The sort of price paid by people like Bernard, Lydia and Eleanor, and the fictitious Nancy, can give us a clue to this cost. But the suffering and sacrifice of Jesus has to be immeasurably deeper and darker. They each suffered for an individual they loved: Jesus suffered for us all. Mere man can never do this: only God could bear such a weight and accomplish such a mission. Christians claim that, in Jesus Christ, mysteriously and marvellously God and man became one to work this miracle; so it was possible for St Paul to write, 'Christ's love compels us, because we are convinced that one died for all' (2 Corinthians 5:14).

The sin which is in you and me has lashed out at Jesus and yet, amazingly, he has borne our blow and continues to offer that relationship of love and forgiveness which alone can save and change us. He has died at our hands and then risen again, still loving us.

And the resurrection was followed by the ascension – a

vital transition. From his birth until his ascension Jesus was only in one place at a time. Only with his ascension did the promise of his omnipresence – 'I am with you always, to the very end of the age' (Matthew 28:20) – become reality.

As I write these words and as you read them, Jesus is with me and Jesus is with you, offering God's forgiveness and assuring us that he has paid the price of our sins: 'The Son of Man did not come to be served, but to serve, and to give his life as a ransom for many' (Mark 10:45). In the lovely words of the hymn by William Young Fullerton:

> I cannot tell how silently He suffered,
> As with His peace, He graced this place of tears,
> Or how His heart upon the cross was broken,
> The crown of pain to three-and-thirty years.
> But this I know, He heals the broken-hearted,
> And stays our sin, and calms our lurking fear,
> And lifts the burden from the heavy-laden,
> For yet the Saviour, Saviour of the world, is *here*.

To all who put their trust in Jesus, St John gives this guarantee: 'If we confess our sins, he is faithful and just and will forgive us our sins and purify us from all unrighteousness' (1 John 1:9).

However, the word 'if' is important. Jesus brings us God's forgiveness. He yearns for us to accept it. He pays the price of his own life so that this forgiveness should be available to us. But he does not force forgiveness upon us. God never violates our free will, not even for our own essential and eternal good. An offer of forgiveness does not mean that you and I are automatically forgiven people. Forgiveness takes two – one who is ready to forgive and one who is ready to be forgiven. We become forgiven people when in prayer we place ourselves at the foot of the cross, acknowledge we are sinners and, in a spirit of penitence, *ask* for forgiveness in the name of Jesus, our Saviour.

Then God's forgiveness floods over us. We enter through the 'Forgiveness gate' into God's church, God's kingdom, God's presence – and life is never the same again.

At this point may I invite you to pause and join me in an act of receiving the forgiveness that Jesus lived, died, rose and ascended to bring to you and me. You may be reaffirming something you have done long ago, or you may be taking your first step into the experience of Christian forgiveness. In either case, I believe the following prayer is full of healing and power:

> Jesus, I know that I am a sinner, and I'm truly sorry
>   for the wrongs I have done.
> But I also know that you love me and gave yourself
>   for me.
> You offer to come into my life, if I will let you in.
> You offer healing for the sins and hurts of my soul.
> You offer to feed me with your own truth.
> Gratefully I accept your offer to be my Saviour, Lord
>   and Friend. I ask for forgiveness. I put my trust in
>   you and want you to work in me, healing me,
>   feeding me, living in me.
> Help me to use my life in your service. Thank you
>   for all you are going to do in me. Amen.

If you have just prayed in this way for the very first time, then welcome to a new state of being and a new way of life. It is hardly possible to exaggerate the importance of the decision you have made. You are still a sinner, but you are a forgiven sinner.

In the words of Sir Winston Churchill, in his speech at the Mansion House, London, on 10 November 1942: 'This is not the end. It is not even the beginning of the end. But it is, perhaps, the end of the beginning.'

A vital part of the Christian journey is that forgiven sinners learn to be channels of forgiveness themselves. It is all part of God's 'fill and spill' policy: the forgiving love with which he fills us must spill over and spill out from us.

First, we must learn to forgive ourselves. Harriet, a Christian woman of high principle, once said to me, 'God may forgive me, but I will never forgive myself for some of the sins I have committed.' It was a noble statement, but it was wrong. In a sense, it was almost blasphemous because she seemed to be claiming to know better than God about the proper way of regarding herself. We are not called to be permissive in our attitude towards ourselves ('My sins do not matter'), but we are certainly called to enjoy forgiveness ('My sins are totally forgiven') and to experience the liberty and healing that forgiveness brings. This liberty and healing will lead us to be channels of forgiveness to the people around us.

I tell the story of Martha in my previous book, *How to pray when life hurts* (Scripture Union, 1993). She was eaten up with arthritis, so she was largely confined to a wheel chair and in continuous pain. She had herself pushed to a Christian healing centre where she asked for prayer. It would seem that her ill health was somehow related to a spirit of unforgiveness – she was freed from her condition only when she discovered a method of prayer that helped her to forgive someone every day until she ran out of people to forgive. She followed up each prayer of forgiveness with a practical act to show that her forgiveness was real: writing a letter, making a phone call, offering a gift, trying to restore a broken relationship.

Many years ago I discovered a practical method of forgiveness-praying – a prayer sequence that encouraged the praying individual to forgive themselves, their parents (even if they were not alive any more), their siblings, spouses and children, their other relatives and in-laws, their employers and co-workers, their neighbours, their church leaders and fellow church members, their teachers and instructors present and past, their friends and their enemies – and finally the one person who had hurt them the most. A fuller account of this prayer sequence is outlined in *How to pray when life hurts*. Such forgiveness-praying may not be easy, but it is full of healing potential. Even when forgiveness is not accepted, we ourselves will be the better for having offered it.

To refuse to forgive can be dangerous. Jethro was engaged in a dispute with one of his neighbours and would neither offer nor accept forgiveness. The quarrel had begun over a minor disagreement connected with the wall that separated their gardens, but after a while the original problem seemed to pale into insignificance. The wall that divided them was now not made of bricks but rather of anger and bitterness, and it blocked any possibility of sensible speech, thought or action. Jethro's wife asked me to visit him because he had a heart condition and she felt his refusal to forgive was killing him. She was right. He would not listen to me, but held on to his anger and bitterness as though they were a precious treasure rather than a fatal poison. But a fatal poison is precisely what they proved to be and, soon afterwards, Jethro died of a massive heart attack.

The joy that forgiveness can both create in us and confer on others has probably never been better illustrated than in the life of Corrie Ten Boom. In her book, *He cares, he comforts*, she recounts how she met a woman who had formerly worked on the staff of the Concentration Camp at Ravensbrück, a so-called 'nurse' who had been brutal to her sister as she was dying. Corrie's first reaction was one of sheer hatred towards this woman and, for a while, she became the prisoner of that hatred. However, by the grace of God, she was able to turn her mind to God's love, to receive it into herself more and more deeply, until that love became more important to her than her own hatred and bitterness. She was able to forgive the nurse and tell her so. Immediately, release and liberation came. She writes: 'It is a joy to accept forgiveness, but it is almost a greater joy to give forgiveness.' As for the nurse, she was so overwhelmed by Corrie's act of forgiveness that she herself became a committed Christian.

Corrie Ten Boom points the way for us. If you and I feel it is impossibly hard to forgive someone who has wronged us, then we must ponder the love and forgiveness which God has given to us, which he brought to us by the pierced hands of our crucified Lord. As we recollect that he died not only for us but also for those we find it hard to forgive, he will enable us to know that we cannot withhold from others what he has won for us at such a cost. If we harden our hearts, we impair our own capacity to receive God's forgiveness. Forgiving and receiving forgiveness are inseparable in the teaching of Jesus (Luke 11:4). We do well not only to speak the words of the Lord's Prayer, but to absorb its teaching as we say, 'Forgive us our trespasses, *as we forgive those who trespass against us.*'

The parable of the unforgiving servant (Matthew 18:21–35) has a strangely modern ring. An employee, who has been guilty of massive financial malpractice, ends up owing his firm billions – a debt he could not repay in a thousand lifetimes. Incredibly, his employer forgives him. But, even more incredibly, the swindler refuses to forgive one of his colleagues for a comparatively insignificant personal debt! His employer gets to hear of this, and the swindler ends up in jail after all. Jesus comments, 'This is how my heavenly Father will treat each of you unless you forgive your brother from your heart' (Matthew 18:35).

Before ending this chapter, I am going to presume to offer two promises.

When we bear a grudge against somebody, in a subtle way we are in their power. But when we achieve an attitude of forgiveness, we break that power, whether our offer of forgiveness is accepted or not. This is the first promise. Test it and watch it work.

The second promise is that those who practice forgiveness find, mysteriously, that the world seems brighter, pleasanter and altogether kinder – which brings us to the next chapter.

Chapter 3

RECEIVING KINDNESS

CHANNELLING KINDNESS

'The heart of the Eternal is most wonderfully kind,' says Frederick William Faber. I used rather to look down on his hymn, 'Souls of men, why will ye scatter?', and supposed that its recurring emphasis on the kindness of God was sentimental and weak. That view, I now realise, was a sign of my immaturity.

It is a central conviction of scripture that kindness is an integral part of the nature of God. For instance, Psalm 103 is an outburst of praise based on a meditation on God's loving-kindness:

Praise the Lord, my soul!
   All my being, praise his holy name!
Praise the Lord, my soul,
   and do not forget how kind he is…

As a father is kind to his children,
   so the Lord is kind to those who honour him.
            (Psalm 103:1–2,13, *Good News Bible*.)

It is interesting to look at depictions of the pagan gods of the ancient world – some represented as ravening beasts with cruel fangs, or birds of prey with vicious talons – and then to read Psalm 103. Quite a contrast! The God of the Old Testament can, of course, be angry with his people, but his anger is meant to lead us back to an encounter with his underlying kindness. The prophet Isaiah puts the two emotions side by side, revealing which is the more inherent in God's character:

> '"In a surge of anger I hid my face for a moment, but with everlasting kindness I will have compassion on you," says the Lord, your Redeemer.' (Isaiah 54:8.)

The New Testament is completely in accord with this emphasis on the kindness that lies at the heart of God. Jesus' whole gospel mission was 'in order that in the coming ages God might show the incomparable riches of his grace, expressed in his kindness to us in Christ Jesus' (Ephesians 2:7). In the lovely words of St Paul's letter to Titus: 'When the kindness and love of God our Saviour appeared, he saved us not because of righteous things we had done, but because of his mercy' (Titus 3:4–5). It is for us to so absorb God's kindness that we begin to reflect it in the world. Jesus teaches that kindness is at the heart of good neighbourliness. Perhaps his best known parable is that of the good Samaritan (Luke 10:36–37). The story is triggered by a question put to him by a teacher of the law – 'Who is my neighbour?'

In the parable the two people, a priest and a Levite, who might have been expected to help the injured man, deliberately 'passed by on the other side' to avoid doing so. They may have had religious grounds for their action – they may have thought he was dead, and to approach a corpse would mean ritual contamination; however, for Jesus, kindness overrode such considerations. The man was finally rescued by a member of a group traditionally regarded as outcasts by Jewish society – the Samaritan.

At the end of his story, Jesus asks, 'In your opinion which one of these three acted like a neighbour towards the man attacked by the robbers?' The teacher of the Law answers, 'The one who was kind to him.' Jesus replied, 'You go, then, and do the same' (*Good News Bible*).

When I was ordained, dozens of people wrote to me offering their prayers and advice. One of these letters has stayed in my mind above all the others. Nearly two years before my ordination, the Hungarian uprising against Soviet domination had taken place. On 25 October 1956 university students demonstrated in the cause of democracy. Huge crowds joined them. They were opposed by the secret police and by Soviet troops who fired on them. But the whole nation seemed to join them, and the Soviet troops withdrew. Non-communists were taken into the government. The democratic parties were reconstituted. Cardinal Mindszenty was released from prison.

Then one week later, on 30 October, Soviet mechanised troops rolled back in. Bodies were crushed under the tank-tracks. The country was immersed in a blood bath. Soviet domination was re-established. However, 160,000 refugees managed to make their escape, and I came to know two of them. Before my ordination one of them wrote to me. I shall never forget his words. He said, 'Teach your people to be kind. Kindness is what this world needs.'

Of course, he was right. What a difference more kindness would make in this world – in the conflict between Arabs and Jews in Palestine; in the genocide that has engulfed Serbs, Croats and Bosnians in what used to be Yugoslavia; in the suffering inflicted on Kurds in Iraq; on the Christian minority in the Sudan; on the dispossessed people in and around Rwanda; and, nearer home, in community relationships in Northern Ireland.

'Teach your people to be kind. Kindness is what this world needs.' This chapter is a small response to that commission.

I invite you to run a 'kindness test' on yourself. It will have two parts, one based on input and the other based on output.

First, let's look at input. Is your idea of God a kind God – the sort of God who would fit the description in Psalm 103 and the verses from Isaiah quoted earlier in this chapter? Or do you have a mental picture of a rather fierce and stern God, a God of judgement and condemnation, a God with a crab-apple face, a God whose approbation has to be won the hard way? Is your God like the forgiving father in the story of the prodigal son (Luke 15:11–24) or is he more like the unforgiving elder brother (Luke 15:25–31)?

If the kindness that, according to Jesus, lies at the heart of God is indeed pouring into us, then this brings us to part two of the kindness test – how well is God's 'fill and spill' policy working within us? How well are we channelling what we receive?

I am privileged to have Hilda in my congregation, and the whole church is privileged to have experienced her remarkable kindness. For years she led a group which provided a monthly luncheon party for the elderly and lonely of our area and a full Christmas Dinner on Christmas Day. She also found time to be a play-group leader and a Sunday School Superintendent. She and her husband Ken have fostered fifty children over the years. Yet she has always found the time and energy to be kind to neighbours in trouble. She is well known for calling on people who have been bereaved, with home-made scones and home-spun sympathy.

In a recent book Russ Parker and I wrote together (*Healing and Evangelism*, SPCK) I was moved to recount an example of Hilda's practical kindness. It was actually happening as the book was being produced...

I am writing this at a time of appalling catastrophe in Rwanda. Thousands of people, many of them little children, are dying week by week. It is a self-inflicted wound, but it would be no help to tell that to the children or to any of the other victims who just happen to be in the wrong place at the wrong time.

What does it mean to be a healing church at a time like this? UNICEF has made an appeal to the churches for prayers and a collection, and so ten days ago we said our prayers and put a collection box at the back of our churches. At the end of the day there was over £200 in the boxes. That completed our involvement – so I thought. But I reckoned without God and without a member of our congregation called Hilda.

Hilda came to me at the back of the church and I told her, perhaps a little smugly, that we had over £200 in the box. 'It won't do,' she said very quietly but firmly. 'I believe that God has told me we must send £1,000 and send it now. If you will ask the treasurer to send £1,000 now, I will guarantee that the other £800 will come from somewhere.'

The churchwardens and I hovered about her rather uncertainly. We do give a tenth of our income away in any case, but £800 would make a hole in this amount, and we did not want to reduce the sum we had planned to send to other good causes.

'How about £500, Hilda?' I asked tentatively. Gently she answered, 'When God says £1,000 we can't offer him less.'

Another church member said, 'Perhaps £600?'

'One thousand pounds,' said Hilda.

I obtained the cheque for £1,000 and took it to Hilda. 'Are you sure about this?' I asked.

'I'll post it' she answered, and so she did.

Before next Sunday, people had come from all over the parish to Hilda's front door with cheques and bank notes. Within a week we had a thousand pounds and, as I write a few days later, we are well on our way to another thousand!

In fact, we were able to send well over £2,000 to the UNICEF and Christian Aid appeals, and it was all due to Hilda.

Year after year I have tried to obtain some recognition for Hilda in the national honours list. Year after year I have failed. She isn't important enough for our politicians to notice her. But she is certainly important to the sick, the needy and the lonely, to the very old and the very young, and I am sure she is important to God.

She will be embarrassed to read this. Perhaps you and I are embarrassed too, but for a different reason. Perhaps we realise how little of this could be said about us. If so, what can we do? It may well be useless to seek to dredge an ounce or two of extra kindness out of the murk of our selfish souls, to strain to be more sympathetic and push ourselves towards greater practical care. It is better to begin at the beginning, to remember the input/output principle.

Why not make a detailed list of the ways in which you have experienced God's goodness? You might start by remembering the gospel gift itself, God's gift of Jesus. 'God so loved the world' – and that means you and me – 'that he gave his only-begotten Son.' He gave him in the cradle, he gave him on the cross, so that you and I could sing:

Jesus, kind above all other,
Gentle child of gentle mother,
In the stable born our brother,
Give us grace to persevere.

Jesus, for thy people dying,
Risen Master, death defying,
Lord in heaven, thy grace supplying,
Keep us to thy presence near.

(Adam of St Victor, twelfth century.)

Having pondered the incredible kindness of God's gift of Jesus, you can then recollect your more personal reasons for gratitude, not forgetting to thank God for kindness from innumerable human sources, perhaps including some unlikely ones.

Georgina, one of my congregation, told me a lovely story of an unexpected kindness. Her car had broken down on a dark, wet night. She tried to attract the notice of passing cars, but none would stop for her. Then, with a sense of chill, she realised that a menacing figure was walking towards her – a solitary young man, dressed in black leather covered in metallic studs. She tried to stop a few more cars and was drenched with water from a puddle as they drove past ignoring her. As her object of fear came closer, she could see he was long-haired and unshaven. Finally, he came right up to her and stopped.

'Are you in trouble, love?' he asked. 'Why don't you get in your car and I'll give you a push?'

In the event, he pushed her all the way to her home three roads away and, when she tried to give him some money, he wouldn't accept. 'It's a poor world if you can't give a helping hand,' he said and went off whistling.

How many expected and unexpected acts of kindness can

you count in your own life? It's a good exercise and, in the light of the input/output principle, it is an excellent preparation for asking the question 'If I look back over the past seven days, how many acts of kindness have *I* actually done myself?'

Remember the question Jesus asked at the end of the parable of the good Samaritan: 'Which one of these acted like a neighbour?' The answer: 'The one who was kind.' And Jesus' final comment: 'You go, then, and do the same.'

Chapter 4

RECEIVING GOD'S LOVE

CHANNELLING GOD'S LOVE

Kindness is a lovely quality, but love is lovelier still. Love has been sung about, written about and romanticised throughout the centuries. 'Let's live and love,' wrote the poet Catullus in the days of the Roman Empire. In the twentieth century Cole Porter has said the same thing in his own inimitable way:

> Birds do it, bees do it,
> Even educated fleas do it,
> Let's do it, let's fall in love!

These are just two of over 600 references to love in *The Oxford Dictionary of Quotations*, yet love proves an elusive word if you try to define it. In his book, *The Four Loves*, C S Lewis tells us that the English word 'love' is represented by four words in Greek.

The first is *storge* (pronounced 'store-gay') and refers to family affection. This is a common and natural feeling found in animals as well as human beings. Animals will sometimes risk their lives for the sake of their young: even a sheep – which is hardly equipped to fight – may do so to defend her lambs.

I recently conducted the funeral of a lovely woman. She died at the age of 91, after caring first for her elderly mother and then her brother when he became an invalid; then she nursed her sister-in-law when she became ill; she then took responsibility for her sister who died aged 95; and, finally, she insisted on providing for all her own needs, so as not to be a trouble to any other members of the family. One of the older men in my parish also spent many years selflessly looking after his disabled wife until she died. When I told him how much I admired him, he was surprised. 'You've got to look after your own,' he said, and to prove it he then took an elderly aunt into his home.

Storge is an important and noble quality, but it can go wrong. It can become exclusive, indifferent to any outside the family circle – as in the case of the farmer whose prayer Ronald Brown, former bishop of Birkenhead, used sometimes to quote at confirmation services:

> God bless me, Lord,
> And my wife, Maud,
> And our son, Sam,
> And his wife, Pam,
> Us four,
> No more!

Love is clearly more than that, so on to the second Greek word, *philia* (pronounced 'fillia'), the love which friends have for each other.

The television series *Last of the Summer Wine* provides good examples of friendship in Compo, Clegg and Foggy. There is a fair amount of *philia* in other programmes too –

as fans of *Casualty* or *The Bill* or *Star Trek* will know. There are books about *philia* too, like the three musketeers of Alexandre Dumas, with their motto 'All for one and one for all'; or Conan Doyle's Sherlock Holmes and Dr Watson; or Agatha Christie's Poirot and Hastings; or David and Jonathan in the Bible.

However, once again there is danger that others outside the circle of friends might be excluded. A close-knit group can degenerate into a clique, a gang, an inner ring. Have you ever walked into a room full of friends and felt a total outsider?

The third Greek word *eros* (usually 'eeross' as in the statue of Eros, though the correct pronunciation is 'errose') is used to define sexual love. This kind of love is a basic ingredient of human nature: it is created by God and intended to lead to the joy of the deepest and closest of human relationships. However, again *eros* can be distorted. In fact, the devil often has a field day because this sort of love can degenerate into lust. It is vital that we know the difference. Love is concerned only for the beloved, whereas lust is self-centred and concerned mainly about its own pleasurable sensations. Love is creative, lust is destructive, spawning unhappiness and disease. If this distortion is to be prevented, we need now to move to the fourth type of love.

Philia is only used once in the New Testament (James 4:4), and the words *storge* and *eros* do not appear at all. However, a fourth Greek word – *agape* (pronounced 'aga-pay') appears quite often, with reference to both God's love and that of human beings. This is the love at the heart of St Paul's famous hymn in chapter 13 of 1 Corinthians – love which is neither self-centred nor exclusive:

Love is patient, love is kind. It does not envy, it does not boast, it is not proud. It is not rude, it is not self-seeking, it is not easily angered, it keeps no record of

wrongs. Love does not delight in evil but rejoices in
the truth. It always protects, always trusts, always
hopes, always perseveres. (1 Corinthians 13:4–7.)

Agape truly wants the best for others and will give itself
freely for that purpose. If *philia, storge* and *eros* are not to
go wrong, they have to have something of *agape* in them.
When Jesus commands us to love our neighbour as ourselves (Mark 12:31), *agape* is the kind of love he is referring to. This is the sort of love that leads to life at its deepest and best – but there is a snag.

We might find St Paul's rhapsody on love decidedly
depressing – we fall so far short of it ourselves. If I try
putting my own name in place of 'love' in 1 Corinthians 13
('Roy Lawrence is patient. Roy Lawrence is kind. Roy
Lawrence does not envy', and so on) I could never delude
myself that it paints an accurate picture of me! So where do
I go from here? Into self-accusation and self-contempt?
Thankfully not, because once again I can go back to the
input/output principle which is the heart of Christian faith
and life. God's nature is pure *agape* (1 John 4:8). That is our
one and only resource as we seek to grow a little in love day
by day.

Imagine an electrical circuit. Think of your own house.
Electricity comes from the source of supply and flows
around your domestic circuit so that the household gadgets
can work. Now imagine a different sort of circuit – a love
circuit. Love comes from its source, God, and flows
through one person, into another, and another, and another,
and ultimately back to God.

A Christian marriage is meant to be a love circuit. Love
flows from God, through a man, into his wife, and back to
God. It flows through a woman, into her husband, and back
to God. When children come along, they too become part of

the love circuit. And, outside of marriage, all Christian friendship, relationships within the church, should embody the same principle. The good news is that God is infinite and so love can be infinite. If the flow begins to dry up, the gospel tells us not to beat ourselves up over our own limited powers to love, but instead to seek to develop a closer relationship with the Lord of Love. To help us do this, let us meditate now on the ways that God shows his love.

He shows it in creation. Love does not naturally live alone – it seeks others with whom it can share itself. God made us from love and for love. Having created us, he affirmed us: 'God saw all that he had made, and it was very good' (Genesis 1:31).

Sometimes I ask my congregation to say out loud together the words, 'I am a worthwhile person.' Usually their first attempt is a pathetic mumble. But when they have said the words half a dozen times, they begin to say them with conviction, and often end up shouting them. Good news deserves to be shouted aloud, and the good news is that God does not make rubbish! Why not go now to a private place yourself, stand before the affirming love of your Creator and say aloud several times, 'I AM A WORTH-WHILE PERSON!'

After creating us and affirming us, God makes it his business to provide for us. The human race depends totally on God's gifts of food, drink, shelter, medicine and all the other bounties that we glean from the earth. If these were to fail completely for just one year, the greater part of the human race would die. But, in spite of all that we do to the earth, year after year these things remain. What God creates and affirms, he also sustains in his love. In spite of the rising numbers in the world's population, the earth produces enough for everyone. The fact that people do starve is mostly down to our own failure as stewards of God's creation.

God's love goes even further. Humankind turned away from God and put self on God's throne in response to the serpent's seductive temptation, 'You will be like God' (Genesis 3:5). Yet God's response was, amazingly, to come and live among us as one of us, in Jesus Christ. The miracle of creation, affirmation and provision, was followed by the miracle of identification. Identification with sinners like us required the ultimate sacrifice.

This too was the gift of love.

My song is love unknown,
My Saviour's love to me:
Love to the loveless shown,
That they might lovely be.
O who am I, that for my sake
My Lord should take frail flesh and die?

He came from his blessed throne
Salvation to bestow;
But men made strange, and none
The longed-for Christ would know:
But O! my Friend, my Friend indeed,
Who at my need His life did spend.

(Samuel Crossman.)

This love is our supreme resource for loving. As it spills from him and into us, sooner or later the input/output principle must begin to apply:

See from His head, His hands, His feet,
Sorrow and love flow mingling down:
Did e'er such love and sorrow meet,
Or thorns compose so rich a crown?

Were the whole realm of Nature mine,
That were an offering far too small;
Love so amazing, so divine,
Demands my soul, my life, my all!

                    (Isaac Watts.)

Even ordinary human love has a fill-and-spill effect on us. Brenda was a forewoman at a clothing factory. The girls who worked under her found her very difficult – a sour, unsmiling martinet. Then quite suddenly she changed. She became friendly, helpful and happy. Nobody could understand it until one day one of her girls noticed the engagement ring on Brenda's finger. Brenda was just reacting to the experience of being loved. At the heart of the Christian faith is the conviction that God engaged himself, covenanted and committed himself to love you and me. That is the message of the acts of creation, affirmation, provision, identification and sacrifice which stem from his love.

Lovers used to play a game, pulling petals off a flower. She loves me, she loves me not, she loves me, she loves me not – and so on till all the petals were gone. With God I need only one petal – HE LOVES ME. Love is God's nature, and you and I are privileged to rest in that love. Resting in that love we can begin to be its channel – we can begin to be creative; we can affirm, provide for and identify with others. We may even begin to love sacrificially. But we should not attempt to do this in our own strength.

Make me a channel of your peace,
Where there is hatred, let me bring your love.

The operative word is 'your'!

Chapter 5

RECEIVING HEALING

CHANNELLING HEALING

There is no better example of the input/output principle than that provided by the ministry of Christian healing. The basis of Christian healing is the practice of the presence of Jesus Christ. When Christians worship together we claim Jesus' promise: 'Where two or three come together in my name, there am I with them' (Matthew 18:20). His presence stays with us from day to day. We have his Ascensiontide pledge for it: 'I am with you always to the very end of the age' (Matthew 28:20). Jesus has not changed. He is 'the same yesterday and today and for ever' (Hebrews 13:8). It is therefore no more than simple logic to expect that an encounter with him today will have the same healing potential as is so evident in his earthly ministry.

There can be no doubt about the healing content of that ministry. To Jesus, healing was as central as teaching and preaching: he 'went throughout Galilee, teaching in their synagogues, preaching the good news of the kingdom and healing every disease and sickness among the people' (Matthew 4:23). There were instances of mass healing (eg Matthew 14:14) and of individual healing – blindness (Matthew 9:27–31), deafness (Mark 7:31–35), lameness (Matthew 11:4–5), paralysis (Matthew 8:5–13), fever (Matthew 8:14–15), skin conditions (Matthew 8:1–3), and so on. No physical condition seemed to be exempt from Jesus' influence. However, his healing ministry was much wider than the physical. Mental and spiritual conditions responded to his presence, sometimes in quite spectacular ways (eg Luke 8:26–39; 9:37–43). Lives were transformed (eg Matthew 9:9–13; Luke 19:1–10). Those who opened themselves to his influence were never the same again.

We should not be surprised if this happens today. If Jesus truly made a healing difference in body, mind and spirit to people whom he encountered during his earthly ministry, and if he is truly risen and available today, and if he is 'the same yesterday, today and for ever', logically we should not be surprised if there is a healing ministry today when Christians claim his promised presence. Logically, we should be surprised if there is no healing at all!

So it is that today's church is rediscovering the Christian healing ministry. Of course, there is a danger of error and excess as we do, but gradually a sensible scriptural healing ministry is becoming an element in the life of more and more ordinary churches, and I for one praise God for it.

I have known many instances of Christian healing. Some are major events relating to seemingly incurable conditions, such as multiple sclerosis or cancers which have been pronounced terminal. Some relate to lesser conditions. God is concerned about all sorts and conditions of life, both great and small. There is no space to repeat them all here, but it may perhaps be helpful if I give some personal experience of ways in which the healing presence of the Lord has made a difference to my wife, Eira, and myself. I have already written about Eira's physical healing back in 1979 (in

Invitation to Healing, InterVarsity Press [US]), soon after our arrival in our present parish. But I would like to share it again.

Before we were married, when Eira was working as a physiotherapist, she slipped a disc while lifting an eighteen-stone patient. She was off work and in bed for some time and, when she started work again, she was aware of a weakness in her back and of the need to take care.

This weakness was still with her when we married, and it constituted a real problem for her, because being the wife of a vicar is a much more strenuous business than most people realise. For a start there is a large house to care for and usually a large garden thrown in for good measure. Literally hundreds of people have to be entertained during the course of each year. Scores of cups of tea and coffee are brewed for callers, who can range from visiting bishops to visiting tramps. Sometimes the church's guests have to be entertained overnight or for a longer period. When the church, or the church hall, needs spring-cleaning it falls to the vicar's wife to lead the bucket-and-mop brigade. The vicarage phone and door bell ring with frightening frequency. The call could be someone wanting to demonstrate a new product for cleaning the church floor. It could be someone wanting to arrange a christening, a wedding or a funeral. It could be a couple with a marriage problem, or someone feeling suicidal who decides to try religion as a last resort before putting his or her head in a gas oven. On such occasions the odds are that I will be out at a service or a meeting, or out visiting in the parish. So whatever the problem is, more often than not, Eira is landed with it. And simultaneously, of course, the life of the family has to go on.

We are sometimes told that our vicarage has an atmosphere of peace and tranquillity. A miracle in itself! But after a while it became clear that the peace and tranquillity which others found was taking its toll on Eira. While we were at Hyde, her back began to give renewed trouble and, year after year, the problem increased. She had to have days in bed, then a week, then a fortnight. Often her movements were stiff and painful, and she said that she felt ninety-nine years old. A check X-ray showed continued narrowing of the disc spaces; but seeing the trouble was one thing, healing it was another.

In vain Eira tried the various exercises on herself which she knew so well as a physiotherapist. In vain we prayed for her healing and I administered a laying on of hands in the Lord's name both in church and at home. In theory Eira believed in Christian healing: it made sense to her as a physiotherapist and as a Christian. But in practice she grew steadily worse, and she began to fear she might turn into a permanent invalid.

Then we were asked to move from Hyde to Birkenhead, and our hearts failed us when we saw what was to be our next home. The vicarage at Hyde had been reasonably large, but it paled into insignificance beside Prenton vicarage. Ten bedrooms! Twenty-eight rooms altogether! What a load to put on Eira's creaking back. The church council was marvellous and, as an act of faith, authorised the spending of thousands of pounds – which they did not have – on modernising and improving the house as far as possible. We believed it was the place where God wanted us to be. But Eira was filled with trepidation as we moved in. She prayed, 'Lord, it all seems impossible to me. I don't see how I can cope. If you are calling us to this new work, you will have to cope for me.'

Praise be, God did just that! Some months after our arrival in Prenton, one Sunday evening after our monthly service of Christian healing, as Eira was having a bath, quite suddenly she knew she was healed. She stepped out of the bath and, for the first time in eighteen years, she touched her toes.

The difference in her now is most remarkable. For years I had carried the tea-tray from the kitchen to the sitting room because it hurt Eira's back. Suddenly she was able to carry it herself without trouble. If anything, life has become more exacting than ever for her, but she finds she can put her new back into it without harm. On the occasions when we have spent afternoons together cleaning up our massive garden, I am the one who has collected any back-aches that were going, not Eira. She has a degree of supple movement now that I have never known in her before.

Eira's healing proved long-lasting and complete. As she and I have reflected on it during the course of many years, we can find no reason for it happening other than the active healing presence of our Risen Lord Jesus at the heart of Christian worship.

Over time I have become aware of a healing of my own, no less wonderful to me than that of Eira's back. In my case the healing has been emotional and spiritual rather than physical. In my early years I was a deeply anxious child. Insecurity was my constant companion. It is a horrid and debilitating state of mind. I believe that its roots can be identified in some of my very first experiences of life, but knowing this does not necessarily bring freedom. At school, bullies sensed my fearfulness and found me a natural target. I also felt myself a prisoner in the road where my family lived – at each end there was a dog, an Alsatian at one end and a bouncy jumping wire-haired terrier at the other. Both of them were a source of great fear to me.

However, as I learned to sense and to affirm the presence of Christ in my life, gradually he lifted this fearfulness from my soul. I am now amazed how little anxiety there is in me. One of the results can be seen in what has happened to my one-time dog phobia. When I was ordained, I knew that it would be a major disadvantage if, on every occasion I visited a house with a dog in it, I found myself petrified. So I asked our Lord to enable me to tolerate dogs, to bear their presence without cringing. Dogs tend not to like people who are afraid of them, and all dog-owners tend to think their pets are great judges of character!

Then my little miracle happened. Not only was my fear of dogs taken away, but I started actually *liking* them. Now I absolutely adore them. I feel that every dog in my parish belongs to me, and many of the dogs seem to be of the same mind.

The disappearance of my dog-phobia is a symptom of a greater healing. Over the years Jesus has given me the conviction that, because God has made me and loves me and has called me into his service, I have no right to be fearful. 'Do not be afraid' is a scriptural command, occurring on seventy-nine different occasions in the Bible. I believe that whatever God commands he also enables, in and through Jesus Christ. This is my experience of Christian healing, and I can testify to the reality of it and to the difference it has made. It would have been difficult to do the work of a minister without it. Often in the ministry one sometimes has to take an unpopular decision, say something that people don't want to hear, or confront someone with an unpalatable truth. I could not do it if I were paralysed by anxiety and insecurity or hiding behind some debilitating defence mechanism. I thank God it has been proved to me in practical terms that 'where the Spirit of the Lord is there is freedom' (2 Corinthians 3:17).

These gifts of healing have come to Eira and to me as part of the input that Jesus has had in our lives. You may well be able to tell a similar story from your own life and experience.

Here again we come to the gospel principle that input and output should go together. I am called not just to be a receiver but also to be a channel of Christ's healing, and so is every believer. Believers are the 'body of Christ' (1 Corinthians 12:27), experiencing union with Jesus and therefore enabled to speak his word, to do his work and to convey his healing. This was the commission of Jesus to his followers (eg Luke 9:1–2,6; 10:1,9) and it has never been withdrawn.

It was when I became convinced of this that I started to hold Christian healing services as a regular ingredient in the worship-programme of my church. These services have now been a monthly event for twenty-five years, and the healing ministry has become an integral element in pastoral visiting and parish life as a whole. I cannot now conceive of Christian ministry without it and, over the years, my colleagues and I have been involved in literally hundreds of occasions when we have seen the healing power of Christ in action in the bodies, minds and spirits of all kinds of people. And this has happened in spite of the fact that not one of us would claim to have a special 'gift' of healing. Jesus *is* himself the gift. If we are one with him, we can all find our own appropriate ways of channelling Jesus' healing.

Because she is a chartered physiotherapist, my wife Eira has been led to devise a method of combining physical and spiritual relaxation. She calls it 'Time out with God'. Many have told us that it has proved an effective channel of Jesus' healing power.

Glynis is a hairdresser who found herself increasingly suffering from neck and shoulder pains, brought on by years of bending over her clients. It interfered with her work by day and her sleep by night. These pains were healed at a Christian healing service. As she reflected on her healing, and on the fact that her own work involved her in 'laying hands' on people continually, she decided that from then on she would link her hairdressing with a ministry of prayer. Nobody knew what she was doing, but it was not long before people started to tell her how much better they felt after their perm or set.

I know a lovely couple whose home has become a virtual centre of Christian healing. They are hospitable by nature. However, because they are committed Christians, they not only offer love and care to a stream of visitors, they also offer Jesus, sharing the gospel in word *and* deed. Many a bruised life has benefited in consequence, including my own.

Strangely, even our disabilities can sometimes become a channel of healing when our lives have been touched by Jesus. When I finish writing this chapter, I shall be going to give a talk at a luncheon meeting of our local 'Daylight' group. Daylight is an organisation that started in our parish but is beginning to spread beyond it. It was formed by a group of people who all suffered from forms of chronic sickness. None of them have as yet received physical healing from their disabilities, but they have discovered that they have the power to communicate with others who suffer from chronic illness. As they do so, they bring hope, encouragement and support in the name of Jesus. Daylight's founder members are all committed to the Christian healing ministry, and they are becoming increasingly effective channels of that ministry.

Whatever our present condition of life, Jesus invites us all to put one hand into his and then, with the other, to extend the offer of his healing touch to the world.

Chapter 6

RECEIVING TRUTH

CHANNELLING TRUTH

It is no secret that these days most churches and chapels in Britain are *not* packed to the rafters with worshippers. It is not that the population as a whole would like to see the churches disappear: the British countryside would not be the same without churchyards, spires and stained-glass windows. They are enjoyed for their aesthetic value and for the contribution they make to our heritage. And many people would be quite upset if churches and chapels were not available for weddings, christenings and Christmas carol services.

So why do most of the population stay away on the average Sunday? I know the sort of reasons that are often given. I also know that these reasons often contradict each other. 'The services are boring – they're too traditional.' But, on the other hand, 'You can't find a traditional service these days – it's all gimmicks and guitars!' Or 'The church is out of date and narrow minded.' But then 'The church is wishy-washy and has nothing to say. It has abandoned its standards!'

It would seem that the church can't win, whatever it does and says, and I believe there is a good reason for this. I think many of these criticism are smoke-screens rather than genuine reasons for staying away. To stick my neck right out, I believe many stay away because they *are afraid of God's truth* and they have a sneaking suspicion that they may just happen to hear it in God's church! Jesus certainly found that the truth was unwelcome in his day. People flocked to him in the hope of seeing a miracle; but when they heard his truth, they deserted him in droves (eg John 6:60–66) and eventually crucified him.

In fact we are foolish to resist God's gospel truth. Though it may often cause us discomfort, it can also be a source of comfort, and it is all for our good. We need the truth quite desperately. In the last chapter I spoke of three profound truths which have brought me great comfort and freedom from fear at a time of emotional and spiritual need. These are worth considering in greater depth.

• *God made me*

I am not some casual bit of flotsam or jetsam which the universe has thrown up by accident. I have been carefully made by a wonderful Creator, and so have we all.

After God created the mineral, vegetable and animal kingdoms, he is represented as saying the mysterious words, 'Let us make man in our own image, in our own likeness' (Genesis 1:26). I wonder why the plural – 'us' and 'our' – is used here. Since we are made in God's image, and there is only one of him, who are these others God is referring to? The explanation usually given is that this is an expression of the fullness and community that exists in the Godhead, an expression that is found in the plural Hebrew word regularly used for God – *elohim*. I accept this as an important truth, though I believe it is worth saying that God seems also to be communing here with all he has created thus far. Human beings are to be part mineral, part vegetable, part animal, but also, in a unique way, spiritual – reflecting and participating in God's own nature.

Chemical analysis reveals the 'mineral' side of man. In the average human being there is, so I am told, enough carbon for 9,000 lead pencils, enough phosphorous for 2,200 match heads, enough fat for 7 bars of soap, enough iron for one medium sized nail, enough lime to whitewash a chicken coop, plus small quantities of magnesium and sulphur, all mixed with 10 gallons of water!

However, there is more to man than that. When, in *Star Trek*, a space-robot describes human beings as 'carbon-units', the description is clearly inadequate. We share life with flowers, trees and grass, and sometimes may actually experience a sense of kinship with that life when from a hilltop we survey the stunning panorama below, or wonder at the fragile beauty of a rose. We also share in the more complex life of the animal kingdom. We are in James Herriot's debt for reminding us in his books of the extraordinary empathy that some humans can achieve with the animals in their care.

Yet, having said this, there is much more to human nature. The animal, vegetable and mineral worlds may all have had a hand in our creation, but humanity is somehow greater in its essence and in its potential: 'God created man in his own image, in the image of God he created him' (Genesis 1:27); 'God is Spirit' (John 4:24), and we are spiritual. The importance of this cannot be exaggerated. In the words of William Temple, 'If man is spiritual and the stars are not, then God is vastly more concerned about the selfishness of a child than about the wreck of a solar system'. This thought brings us to the second profound truth.

• *God loves me*

Because of our affinity with the animal, vegetable and mineral kingdoms, St Francis of Assisi was right to speak of 'our sister water', 'our brother fire' and 'our mother earth'. But, amazingly, Christians are also invited to speak of 'our Father God'. You and I are immeasurably precious to God who offers himself to us as our Father. We do not have to earn his love: it is rooted in his own deep nature. This is his greatest gift and our greatest privilege. It is the rock of our security and the ground of our being. From it stems an invitation to a life of adventure.

This leads on to the third profound truth.

• *God wants me*

God calls me to himself. He has something for me to do and to be. Should I fail to do and to be what God has in his mind and heart for me, then part of God's eternal purpose would be eternally unfulfilled.

God invites us to be involved in both input and output. It is a revealing experience to take a Bible concordance and look up some of the great input words in God's call: 'Come', 'See', 'Taste', 'Rest', 'Abide', 'Eat', 'Drink', 'Receive'. It is equally revealing to look up some of the great output words that are part of God's call: 'Go', 'Do', 'Stand', 'Serve', 'Fight', 'Follow', 'Obey'.

God made me. God loves me. God wants me. To miss these truths is, I believe, to cut ourselves off from healing and wholeness and profound comfort. However, there are also truths in the Christian faith that will cause us profound *dis*-comfort. These too must be absorbed if we are to be whole people.

We have already seen that humankind is a fallen and fallible species. Each one of us is a sinner, a breaker of God's laws: 'If we claim to be without sin, we deceive ourselves and the truth is not in us' (1 John 1:8). The Church of England's *Book of Common Prayer* hammers home this teaching relentlessly in the words of the general Confession:

> Almighty and most merciful Father; We have erred, and strayed from thy ways like lost sheep. We have followed too much the devices and desires of our own hearts. We have offended against thy holy laws. We have left undone those things which we ought to have done; And we have done those things which we ought not to have done; And there is no health in us. But thou, O Lord, have mercy upon us, miserable offenders...

When I first began to go to church, I thought in my immaturity that all this was something of a joke. I did not feel myself to be a 'miserable offender'. I remember coming across a picture postcard on the front at Blackpool. On it was a cartoon of a stout lady kneeling in church, revealing quantities of underwear as she did so. The caption was, 'We have left undone those things which we ought to have done!' I thought it very funny.

But sin is no laughing matter. As we saw in chapter two, sin puts us in deadly peril, both globally and individually, and the evidence for its baleful existence at the heart of fallen human nature is plain to see. There is the evidence of human history. Throughout the centuries humankind has talked peace – but made war. We have praised love – but practised selfishness. This pattern is revealed in the media – again and again the bad news always seems to outweigh the good. In a curious way we even like to have it so. A newscaster once told me that when establishing the priority of news items, the question often asked is 'How much blood?' We find it curiously titillating to be shown what is wrong with the world.

Further evidence of the prevalence of sin is provided by

comparing ourselves with that which is truly good. We have already seen how badly we fare if we assess ourselves in the light of the teaching about life at its best – Jesus' two-fold summary of the Law (Mark 12:31) or St Paul's hymn to Christian love (1 Corinthians 13:4–7). We come off worse if we compare ourselves with truly good people, and especially with Jesus himself.

Evidence of our sinful human nature lies in the fate that frequently befalls the best of the human race. It is a sad fact that many who strive to bring about good suffer imprisonment or death as a result. They are, as we sometimes say, 'too good for this world'. So Alexander Solzhenitsyn endured long years of imprisonment for his protest against Soviet labour camps. Martin Luther King fell victim to an assassin's bullet. And recently in the UK a priest with an urban ministry in Liverpool was murdered in the course of trying to help someone in his parish. During the same week two others also suffered violent attacks.

All over the world journalists, community leaders, campaigners for justice and pastors are jailed or killed for their work to expose evil and make the world a better, fairer place. And Jesus was crucified. You would have to have your eyes and ears firmly shut to avoid the conclusion that there is a serious problem in this sinful world and that we ourselves are part of the problem. However, we are good at shutting our eyes and stopping our ears. We are so often like the three monkeys who 'see no evil, hear no evil and speak no evil'.

There are other truths which we would rather not hear. We would rather not hear about our weakness, our insecurity, our fear, our suppressed rage, our failures. Yet truth is better than falsehood, and the Christian faith never sets out merely to expose painful truth and leave it at that. With the bad news about our sins and follies comes the good news of forgiveness, the revelation of God's love, the offer of healing, freedom, hope, faith and joy – all available in and through Jesus Christ.

Jesus says, 'I am the way and the *truth* and the life' (John 14:6). I believe that if we pursue truth, sooner or later we must find our way to Jesus. And if we commit ourselves to Jesus, we must also commit ourselves to truth. Christians are called to walk Christ's way, live Christ's life and accept Christ's truth, both receiving these things and being the means by which others receive them.

Many years ago I read a book on how to achieve success in life. Its advice was that, if you want to get on in this world, you must never speak an unpleasant truth to those who are above you. Truth, we were told, must be a sacrifice to tactics. But Christians cannot accept this advice without betraying our Lord and ourselves.

Once when I was visiting a former bishop of Chester in connection with a broadcast in which we were both involved, quite suddenly out of the blue he asked me whether I thought he was handling the diocese well or not. He was a man I respected and loved, but I happened to think that he was making a fundamental mistake at the time. It was not easy, but I took a deep breath and told him so!

The result was electric. He jumped out of his chair, paced about the room, waved his hands in the air, prodded me in the chest, went red in the face and generally showed himself far from pleased. I began to envisage my demotion to a perpetual curacy at the far end of the diocese.

Then unexpectedly he stopped and said, 'I'm grateful to you, lad. Others tell me what they think I want to hear. You have told me what you believe is true. We'll have a sherry together.' And we had two or three.

Maybe I was a bit impertinent, but I was not false. A false friend is no friend at all.

Quite a few people will find the truth offensive. Certainly some will find gospel truth offensive. On one occasion, in a former parish, I had to conduct a large civic funeral. As I looked out on the sea of faces, which included many prominent citizens who rarely came to church, I knew I had to offer them the simple truths of the gospel. Afterwards, one of them was livid. As he left, he said 'I will never enter this church of yours again.'

But he was wrong. A fortnight later he entered in his own coffin at his own funeral. I hope he had time to think about the gospel truth to which he had taken such strong objection. I would have failed him totally if that truth had not been expressed.

In chapter three I mentioned the two Hungarian refugees I had met after the abortive uprising there, and told how one of them had written to me before my ordination about the importance of kindness. After I had been ordained for some time, the other also wrote to me. She drew me a picture of a golden flame, which is even now sitting on my desk. Under the flame is this text from Matthew's Gospel, chapter 5, verse 14: 'You are the light of the world. A city that is set on a hill cannot be hid.' She longed for freedom, but she knew that the light of truth has to shine in order that freedom may become a possibility. Jesus said, 'If you hold to my teaching, you are really my disciples. Then you will know the truth and the truth will set you free' (John 8:31–32).

It is not easy to speak unwelcome truth. We do not like to hurt those we love and, when faced with a world that is hostile to truth, fear can easily make us tongue-tied. But if we are receiving and channelling God's love in any real sense, then we have the promise that this perfect love will cast out our fear (1 John 4:18). May God grant us the love and freedom to be both receivers of truth and revealers of truth.

Chapter 7

RECEIVING FREEDOM

CHANNELLING FREEDOM

St Paul promises, 'Where the Spirit of the Lord is, there is freedom' (2 Corinthians 3:17). But what kind of freedom does he mean? Freedom to be myself is the basic answer, and it is an answer with many facets.

We have already thought about the way in which the knowledge of forgiveness brings us a new degree of freedom to admit our own sinfulness. The pretences which adhere so readily to human nature do us no good. It is liberating to be able to come before our gracious God and to say, 'I have broken your laws and sinned against your love. I admit my faults, my failings, my folly. I need your forgiveness in the name of Jesus, my Saviour.' It is liberating to speak these words and know that we do so to the God who loves to say 'Yes'.

There is, of course, a real difference between the 'Yes' of Christian forgiveness and the 'Yes' of worldly permissiveness. They should never be confused. Worldly permissiveness says, 'Yes, this is how you are, and there is nothing wrong with it. Let sin abound.' And not only does sin abound but we remain bound by it. By contrast, Christian forgiveness says, 'Yes, this is how you are, and it is *not* how God means you to be. But take heart – God loves you and, in Jesus, forgiveness, healing and freedom are available.'

God's freedom enables us to admit our weakness. We can spend our entire lives pretending to be strong, but the pretence serves only to increase our sense of weakness deep inside ourselves. A children's parable may help us explore this truth.

A mouse lived in a house which was patrolled by a large and vicious cat with sharp teeth and cruel claws. The mouse was terrified of the cat and spent most of his time hiding in his hole. Eventually he was so frightened that he put up a notice outside his hole, with the words 'Beware! Here lives a big, strong, powerful, aggressive guard-dog'. Then he blocked up the hole, barricading himself inside.

When the cat saw the sign, he avoided going anywhere near the hole. But so did the other mice who might have been the mouse's friends!

The mouse hid away in the darkness on his own till he ran out of provisions. He became too weak to remove the blockade and come out. As he lay dying, the thought came to him – too late – that, though the outside world certainly had its dangers, it was also a source of light and life. Perhaps he should have taken the risk...

The Christian faith gives us permission to be inadequate. We do not have to be the great 'I am': only God can be that (Exodus 3:14). We can accept our limitations and even, in the simple prescription of Dr Brian Lake, 'Enjoy being inadequate'. Then, paradoxically, we find that Jesus helps us to broaden our horizons and push out our parameters. With him we can allow new experiences, new gifts and new strengths to take us by surprise.

Another Christian privilege is the freedom to acknowledge

anger – *even when it is anger against God.* I love the words of Joy Riordan: 'God is a very safe person to be angry with'. The following is a true story which I recounted in my earlier book *How to pray when life hurts*.

A hospice-patient asked to see the chaplain because he was in great emotional distress. The patient was in the last stages of cancer and was feeling very guilty because he had spent the previous night ranting, raving and swearing at God. The following morning he felt dreadful. He imagined that his chances of eternal life had now been lost for ever. Surely God would never forgive someone who had so cursed and abused him.

After listening to his fears, the chaplain asked the patient, 'What do you think is the opposite of love?'

The man replied, 'Hate.'

Very wisely, the chaplain replied, 'No, the opposite of love is indifference. You have not been indifferent to God, or you would never have spent the night talking to him, honestly telling him what was in your heart and mind. Do you know the Christian word that describes what you have been doing? The word is 'prayer'. You have spent the night praying.'

This insight completely changed the attitude of the hospice patient. Not long after his conversation with the chaplain, he died in peace, trusting the God who remains on speaking terms with us even when our only words for him are words of abuse.

This amazing freedom to be honest to God, even when that honesty involves our venting our rage, can be beneficial physically as well as emotionally and spiritually. Recently, I was invited to conduct a seminar on the Christian healing ministry for about thirty people in a housing-estate parish. On our second evening together, I invited seminar members to share personal experiences of Christian healing. One woman told a remarkable story of how a can-cer had vanished after she had told God just how she felt. I commented, 'Yes, prayer can have great healing power.'

After the seminar was over, she waited for some time to speak to me privately and said, 'You did not understand me at all! I was not saying any soothing or respectful prayers when I was healed. I was telling God how I felt, and what I *felt* was anger. I let it all out onto God.'

It was after she had taken her anger out on God that a hospital X-ray could find no trace of her cancer.

Venting our anger in the presence of God is a thoroughly biblical procedure. Moses did it, and so did Elijah, Jonah and Job. There are several instances in the psalms, which is why they make such therapeutic reading when we feel low and depressed. However, the New Testament brings an even more remarkable concept. In our rage, we can hammer the nails into the palms of the Son of God and ram the crown of thorns onto his head; he dies at our hands upon the cross. But then incredibly he rises again – *still loving us*.

This amazing love – this amazing grace – gives us incredible freedom, which can and should enable us to be channels of freedom to others. Because, having granted freedom to you and me, God calls us to help others be free too. In a quite unique way, we are called to be 'freedom-fighters'. This is the object of Christian counselling, Christian listening and Christian friendship.

Of course, Christians should also seek to channel God's freedom to those whose lives are bound and restricted by factors other than psychological and spiritual considera-tions. We are called to bring liberation to those whose lives are threatened or diminished by hunger, disease or persecu-tion. We should work for justice, equality and a fair deal all round. As the saying goes, we must not be so heavenly minded as to be no earthly use, any more than we should be so earthly-minded as to be no heavenly use.

The churches of St Stephen and St Alban in Prenton, of which I am vicar, have formed a link with a church in Maputo, Mozambique. By coincidence, this church is dedicated to St Stephen and St Lawrence! It is a model in the way it combines both heavenly-mindedness and earthly usefulness. In consequence, it brings both new spiritual and new physical freedom to those whose lives it touches.

Mozambique has long been ravaged by warfare and famine. Passions have run out of control and principles set aside, and people have suffered, especially the innocent and vulnerable, those who are very young, very old or very poor. The Christian churches in Mozambique have laboured ceaselessly for justice, compassion and peace. As I write, the situation has mercifully improved in a marked fashion, but there is still so much to do, still so many wounds to heal.

In this situation, the church of St Stephen and St Lawrence has discovered a clear role. Starving children are taken off the streets, fed and taught a simple trade. A divided, violent society is being encouraged to discover the re-creative principles of Christian unity. People in the church are learning to be a living enabling community in the midst of suffering – messengers of freedom, channels of Christ.

Do you and I dare to pause a while and ask ourselves, 'Have I, in any way, a personal equivalent of ministry like that?'

Chapter 8

RECEIVING HOPE

CHANNELLING HOPE

Hope is in distinctly short supply in today's world and understandably so. Scientists now foresee several ways in which life on our planet as we know it could be brought to an end. And even if life on our planet manages to survive, the future prospects of individual nations hardly inspire optimism. People everywhere are experiencing a crisis of personal confidence. Against this background what reasons can we have for a doctrine of Christian hope? What is the nature of this doctrine? Can we hold on to it with any claims to realism?

In seeking an answer to these questions, perhaps a good starting point is that Christians are never promised they will be cushioned and cosseted in this life. Instead the promise we are offered is that, whatever life may bring, somehow 'in all things God works for the good of those who love him' (Romans 8:28).

This *has* to be a logical claim if God is God. When Mother Julian of Norwich says, 'All shall be well, and all shall be well, and all manner of thing shall be well', this is not blind and vapid optimism. She knows about the apparent success story of the forces of sin, but she also knows that, if God exists, then logic requires his ultimate triumph over evil, however menacing the immediate situation may seem to be. The Christian doctrine of hope is part of the Christian doctrine of God. If we believe in God, we can wake up every morning with the question 'How will God surprise me this day?' And we can ask this question no matter how unpromising circumstances may seem.

It is a fact that, in God's world, good comes out of evil again and again. The potential of the undesirable to yield the desirable never ceases to amaze me. I think of the lovely park in Scarborough – built on a rubbish tip. I think of the many occasions on which I have seen people use their experiences of pain, weakness and disaster to bring healing to others. The Daylight group, about which I have already written, is a good example of this. But the crucifixion of Jesus is the best illustration of all. His death could not have been more horrible – brutal, barbaric, breaking every law of natural justice – yet God used it to redeem the world. Death itself does not invalidate the concept of Christian hope. In fact it lends a new dimension to that hope. We shall be thinking about this later.

I remember sitting by the death-bed of a middle-aged woman who was suffering from the last stage of a vicious cancer. With us was another visitor, a very remarkable and much older Christian woman who, because of her own age, could not herself have many years to live. I shall never forget this woman taking the younger woman by the hand and saying, 'Keep looking forward, my dear. Keep looking forward.'

I heard her words with almost a sense of shock, but of course she was right. It is the Christian conviction that wherever we travel with Jesus in this world or the next, we can travel with hope, we can travel with optimism, we can travel with the expectancy that the best is yet to be.

Jesus has a message of hope and encouragement to those who are distressed. He bids us 'Be of good cheer', 'Take courage', 'Take heart', and his message is based on the fact of his presence with us (Matthew 14:23), his pardon (Matthew 9:2) and his peace (John 16:53). The verses behind these words of encouragement are well worth looking up and absorbing prayerfully, because it is a basic Christian claim that the presence, pardon and peace of Christ can be ours too, whatever the external circumstances.

So far I have been writing this chapter against the background of what is sometimes called a 'worst-case-scenario' – global threats, international malaise and personal problems. We have thought about rubbish tips, chronic ailments and incurable disease. But this is far from a balanced picture of life. I have started in this way because if we can live in Christian hope when life seems full of doom and gloom, then there should be no problem when life brings better times and happier experiences.

And it often does. If we follow the advice of the old hymn, 'Count your blessings, count them one by one, and it will surprise you what the Lord has done', we will find that life always has a positive side. In fact because this is a world created and sustained by God, and because the laws of life reflect his own nature, there are many rewards for those who go with the flow of God's will and God's laws.

In the business world and in personal relationships, I believe experience shows that honesty really *is* the best policy. I believe that, by and large, those who love their neighbours stand a better chance of happy relationships than those who don't. Those who follow the Christian sexual code of behaviour are more likely to have healthy bodies and minds than those who ignore it. There is an all-round tendency for wholesome godly living to lead to healthy and happy lives.

It is not unrealistic for Christians to expect God's universe to work with them rather than against them. This too is an ingredient of Christian hope. Moreover, many Christians can tell quite startling stories of the ways in which God sometimes intervenes in answer to prayer, and how a situation can actually change for the better when specifically placed in his hands. It is not that we can make God *serve* us, but when we seek to serve him we may find that we encounter distinctly unexpected blessings. This is yet another element in Christian hope.

As always, we are called not just to experience this hope but also to be the means by which it is channelled to others. Hope can help people help others to think positively rather than negatively, to escape the paralysis that hopelessness brings and to see that, even in times of crisis and catastrophe, it is possible to look for the challenges and opportunities which lie hidden under the surface.

It is sometimes surprisingly easy to be a channel of hope. Let me illustrate this with a story that dates back to my earliest days as a vicar. It was a time when the members of my congregation were feeling distinctly weary. They had worked hard to put new central heating into the church, they had done extensive repairs to the roof and they had raised the money to redecorate the inside of the building. They were ready for a good rest.

It was just at this point that the organ broke down. For many years the organist had kept it going by do-it-yourself repairs to its interior works. The number of bits of string, chewing gum and paper clips which held it together had to be seen to be believed. In the end the strain proved too much, and I was told we needed to raise several thousands pounds to put it into working order.

Psychologically, the timing could not have been worse. A despondent gloom settled on the church officers, and I have to admit that I could not escape it myself. I will never forget how it was dispelled.

One day the vicarage front doorbell rang and, when I answered it, there on the doorstep was a young girl from the junior Sunday School. Let's call her Poppy. She was holding a jam jar full of pennies. She put them into my hands and said, 'I've been saving up and this is to buy the new organ with.'

It seemed a pretty pathetic amount, but I could not help being moved. I thanked her, took the jar of pennies into my study and put it on my desk. Then something strange started to happen. Day after day, I found myself looking at the jar. Poppy and her pennies began to have an affect on me.

A week later, when the PCC met, I took Poppy's jar of pennies and put it where everyone could see it. I told everybody where it had come from and that Poppy wanted us to use it to buy the new organ.

There were several moments of silence while everybody looked at it. Then, one after another, the members started to speak. Amazingly, the fog of depression started to disperse before my eyes. One said, 'I could hold a coffee-morning.' Another said, 'I can hold a strawberry tea.' Pledges of time, talent and money came thick and fast from all over the church hall. In a very short space of time, we had all the money we needed. The new organ was soon in place and sounding out triumphantly. As far as I know, it is still working splendidly.

Poppy gave us more than a jar of pennies. She gave us positivity. She gave us hope. And we can all have our own 'Poppy day!' Even if those around us are experiencing life at its bleakest and blackest, we must never assume there is nothing we can do.

An ex-soldier once told me that after he had been seriously wounded during the D-Day invasion in World War II, he found himself lying amid other wounded men feeling totally lost and hopeless. It was then that an elderly French priest came along, put a hand on his head and said softly, 'Mon pauvre petit' – 'My poor little one'. The ex-soldier told me that, unaccountably, this priest completely lifted his spirits. The empathy in those words, and the tenderness of the touch, became a channel of hope for him. Could God be calling you at this moment to bring the equivalent of Poppy's pennies or the old priest's compassion to someone near you? If so, here are three basic principles for channelling hope:

• *Recognise* that the world is full of problems; it is most unlikely that the little part of the world we are in will be exempt from them. There will be problems in the lives of the people around us, our family, friends, neighbours, workmates. We are called to have open eyes and open hearts to their concerns.

• *Empathise*. Suffer a little alongside those who are in trouble. Avoid easy and glib words. A slap on the back is no help to someone whose back feels as though it is breaking with life's load.

• *Listen to Jesus*. If he is 'the Word' (John 1:1–14), we should expect him to find ways of speaking to us and guiding us.

Finally, in the words of Mary when the wine ran out at the wedding at Cana, 'Do whatever he tells you' (John 2:5). Who knows? He may enable you to do or to say just the thing that brings a shaft of the light of God's healing and hope into someone else's darkness.

Let St Paul have the last word as he expresses his hope that his fellow Christians will be both recipients and channels of Christian hope to the world around them:

> May the God of hope fill you with all joy and peace as you trust in him, so that you may overflow with hope by the power of the Holy Spirit. (Romans 15:13.)

Chapter 9

RECEIVING FAITH

CHANNELLING FAITH

Faith is like a staircase, and this chapter considers seven of the steps. Like everything else in this book, faith is an input/output experience. The further up the steps you go, the greater will be your element of output.

- *Step 1 – Intellectual faith*

Ordinary folk have a sense that there must be some sort of creative force behind this world. Whether you think of the sequence of the seasons or the symmetry of a snowflake, or the beauty of a rose, or the intricate mechanism that allows a human limb to move, let alone the human brain, it seems impossible that the evidence of design can be illusory.

I like the story of the two science lecturers, one of whom was a Christian and the other an atheist. One day, when the atheist was invited to a meal at the other's house, he admired an elaborate working model of the solar system which his colleague had set up in his study. 'That's a marvellous thing,' he said. 'Who made it?' The Christian could not resist answering, 'Well, according to you, it just happened!'

Creation seems to imply a creator, design seems to imply a designer, the laws of cause and effect seem to imply a lawgiver. Where does consciousness come from if the universe is unconscious? Where does personality come from if the universe is impersonal? It does seem all too much to assert over and over and over again that the greater is created by the lesser, and all by accident. Most of us find that our minds will not allow us to be atheists: we need to have some sort of faith in some sort of God.

However, intellectual faith has its limitations, the main one being that any attempt at output on our part is unnecessary. According to St James even devils believe in the existence of God, but this knowledge only makes them shudder (James 2:19)! Before faith can begin to make any real impact on us, we have to mount the second step.

• *Step 2 – Trusting faith*
The difference between intellectual faith and trusting faith was graphically illustrated on the famous occasion when Charles Blondin crossed the Niagara Falls on a tightrope in 1859. He asked the crowd whether they believed he could push a wheelbarrow across the Falls with somebody sitting in it. There was no shortage of those who shouted that they believed it. That was intellectual faith and the crowd had no problem with it. It was when he asked for a volunteer to sit in the wheelbarrow that the difficulty arose! There was a distinct shortage of volunteers then. Ultimately, a woman agreed to get into the wheelbarrow and allow Blondin to push her across the Falls on the tightrope. Hers was trusting faith – and it is good to know that they both made the crossing safely.

I saw a very moving, though rather less spectacular, example of trusting faith in a hotel in North Wales where my family and I once stopped for a meal. There were two disabled people – one blind and the other lame – and they were helping each other walk about the hotel. The lame man trusted the blind man for support, and the blind man trusted the lame man for sight. Because of their trusting faith they got around well.

This is not unlike the trusting faith Christians have in Jesus. We trust his vision of life. We trust the support he offers. Intellectual faith knows that Christians call Jesus Saviour and Lord: but if I have trusting faith I invite him to be *my* Saviour and *my* Lord.

If you found yourself able to make the personal prayer to Jesus on page 20, you have already started along the way of trusting faith and it would be right to describe yourself as a Christian. Progression to the third step of faith will then follow naturally.

• *Step 3 – Sanctifying faith*
This is the faith which makes you a better person, a more wholesome human being, a more complete Christian. It is the faith which shows itself in deeds – a logical and essential progression from trusting faith.

> What good is it, my brothers, if a man claims to have
> faith but has no deeds? Can such faith save him?
> Suppose a brother or sister is without clothes and
> daily food. If one of you says to him, 'Go, I wish
> you well; keep warm and well fed,' but does nothing
> about his physical needs, what good is it? In the
> same way, faith by itself, if it is not accompanied by
> action, is dead. (James 2:14–17.)

The good news is that we do not have to achieve sanctifying faith by our own efforts and in our own strength. It grows within gently by the working of the Holy Spirit.

What is needed on our part is not strain, stress and striving, but only that we *allow* Jesus to have his way. Sanctifying faith comes by our continuing assent to his presence.

All Christians are called to go at least this far up the stairway of faith. But the staircase itself goes further, and God may well be inviting you at this moment to go on to step 4.

- ### *Step 4 – Visionary faith*
Visionary faith sees possibilities that others do not. It sees the opportunities that lie hidden behind problems. Pray that all clergy and church leaders may have visionary faith, and others too. It makes an amazing difference.

Michael was the vicar of a busy town parish. One day he looked out of his vicarage and saw that the church hall was on fire.

The hall burned down to the ground – a major parish disaster. However, it was insured, and not long afterwards Michael, because he is a man of visionary faith, saw an opportunity. Now instead of an old-fashioned church hall there is a modern church-and-community centre. This could not have happened without the disaster, and without Michael's visionary faith.

Mother Teresa looked out on the squalor and poverty of the streets of Calcutta, and her visionary faith showed her that here was an opportunity to do something beautiful for God. She and her work are now famous world wide.

Chad Varah was appalled at the suicide statistics in Britain after the Second World War. Then visionary faith took over. In 1953 he founded the Samaritan movement to help those tempted to suicide and despair. Since then many thousands of lives have been saved, not just in Britain but around the world.

Jean Vanier's concern for the mentally handicapped proved the basis on which his visionary faith founded the

Ark (l'Arche) movement which has established scores of communities around the world. To Jean Vanier the inhabitants of those communities – when seen through the eyes of visionary faith – are people who, though poor in many ways, are possessed of exceptional richness of heart; through their sufferings they reveal to us the inadequacies and poverty of our own lives, and thus help us to live more fully.

God grant that we may all have the eye of visionary faith in circumstances both great and small. But God grant also that our visionary faith may never be fixated at a purely theoretical level. My friend Michael, Mother Teresa, Chad Varah and Jean Vanier all found that visionary faith is not only a step but a springboard to further steps on faith's stairway.

• *Step 5 – Expectant faith*

Expectant faith not only sees the potential within life but expects that, if we pursue God's will, God himself will be with us in the pursuit. Expectant faith gives us the courage and the sheer cheek to have a go.

I think I must confess that for decades my own branch of Christendom, the Church of England, has suffered from dismally low expectancy. The story is told of a communist who attended a traditional Church of England evensong. He was very struck by the words of the Magnificat with its vision of 'scattering the proud in the imagination of their hearts', 'putting down the mighty from their seat' and 'exalting the humble and meek'. After the service he went to the vicar and said, 'That was a marvellous song we sang. What are you going to do about it in your church?' The vicar looked a little embarrassed and could only reply, 'Well, next week we will come back and sing it all over again!'

There is an old cynical saying, 'Blessed are those who

expect nothing, for they shall not be disappointed'. Those who make it their motto will never go far on the staircase of faith.

When Christians are called to worship, we are also called to ask the spine-tingling question, 'What is God going to do with me, in me and through me today?' – a question which may well lead us to …

• *Step 6 – Risk-taking faith*

A friend of ours called Val, a woman with a deep Christian faith, once found herself on the Pleasure Beach at Blackpool watching two youths attacking another. Almost before she realised what she was doing, she went up to them and said, 'In the name of Jesus, stop it!' Amazingly, they stopped. It was only afterwards that it struck her that she had taken quite a risk.

I have heard it said that faith is a word spelt R-I-S-K, and it is certainly true that, as faith progresses, it becomes increasingly difficult to live life in a safe, risk-free fashion. As a matter of personal testimony, I can say that I have never regretted any risks I have taken for God, whereas I have certainly regretted occasions when I have avoided risky living and opted to play things safe. Many a Christian has found that when risks are taken in faith, 'the eternal God is your refuge and underneath are the everlasting arms' (Deuteronomy 33:27).

My wife and I discovered this when we moved to our previous parish. In moving, there we were risking the educational well-being of our two sons because the educational facilities were better where we already were. But (as a missionary-doctor friend reminded us, when we hesitated) God certainly loved our boys no less than we did, and it was amazing how provision was made for their educational needs when we answered what we believed to be God's call.

There were several years when their school fees absorbed the whole of my salary, but neither they nor we ever wanted for anything. Gifts of money and offers of free holidays came to us year after year. Sometimes when we tell this story, we can see that people do not find it easy to believe – but it happened.

We took a different sort of risk when we moved to our present parish. (You have already read this story in chapter five.) God's provision in each case seemed to us to be a minor miracle.

• *Step 7 – Wonder-working faith*

Not everyone is privileged to see a miracle in their life of faith, but I am continually surprised by the number of people who tell me they have done so.

Jesus made this extraordinary statement to his disciples: 'I tell you the truth, if you have faith as small as a mustard seed, you can say to this mountain, "Move from here to there" and it will move. Nothing will be impossible for you' (Matthew 17:20). For my own part, this sort of statement takes me completely out of my depth. Yet every day I still dare to pray the prayer of the Acorn Christian Healing Trust: 'Lord, look upon this work; grant to your servants to speak Your word with all boldness, while You stretch out your hand to heal and signs and wonders are performed, through the name of Your holy servant Jesus' (based on Acts 4:29–30).

For more on faith you may like to study chapter 11 of Hebrews. But, for my part, this description of the staircase of faith must conclude here, not because it comes to an end but because this is where it passes from my vision. However, before concluding this chapter, three final thoughts occur to me.

- The staircase of faith presents a personal challenge. It invites each of us to ask, 'Where am I on faith's staircase? Is it time I moved up a step?'

- It is a distinct and necessary encouragement to me that people who are further up than I am tell me that faith is not so much a staircase as an escalator. In other words, once I pluck up enough courage to step on to it, I can trust God to provide the momentum.

- The journey upwards is never a solitary affair. If we have started the ascent, we will always find people further up than we are, who can offer us help and encouragement. And it is for us in our turn to encourage those still hesitating below us at the bottom.

Chapter 10

RECEIVING JOY

CHANNELLING JOY

When C S Lewis wrote his autobiography, he entitled it *Surprised by Joy*. It is a good title because it is the nature of joy to come as a surprise. I am reminded of the legendary will-o-the-wisp, the little light which is supposed to appear in dark forests and which cannot be caught by pursuit. The more you chase it, the less chance you have of finding it. Joy cannot be caught by pursuit either. It only comes when you are pursuing something else.

Joy is essentially a by-product. In a sense this whole book so far has been about receiving joy. If you receive and channel forgiveness, kindness, love, healing, truth, freedom, hope and faith, I believe you will find that a measure of joy will come with the rest, unsought.

However, we ought to be alert to the fact that many things can serve as deterrents to the presence of joy. For instance, there are the 3 Rs which we need to learn and practice. Lacking any of them will block out joy. They are repenting, restoring and renouncing.

There will be no joy if there is a lack of *repentance*. I do not just mean the repentance which says 'Sorry' to the God we have wronged, but also the repentance which says 'Sorry' to people we have wronged.

The curious science fiction film *Flatliners* makes this point. It tells the story of a group of medical students who undertake an experiment in which for each in turn the physical symptoms of death are induced in an attempt to explore the afterlife. They are then brought back to life so that together they can recall their experiences.

What they discover on the edge of death is that each one needs either to ask someone for forgiveness or to put right a relationship which has gone wrong. One of them tormented a little black girl when he was a boy and is made to realise that he must seek her out and ask for her forgiveness. Another is made to realise how wrong he has been to treat a series of girl friends as no more than sex-objects. Another has to change her attitude to her dead father. And the main character in the film, played by Kiefer Sutherland, had actually killed another boy when he was a boy himself, by merciless bullying. He has to undergo a great deal of suffering and two edge-of-death experiences, in which his own life has to hang in the balance, before he can find atonement and forgiveness.

This, of course, is not a specifically Christian film. It has no concept of sin against God or against life itself, and certainly the Christian concept of salvation through Jesus has no part in it. However, it makes the point that there can be no joy in or beyond this life until we face our need for forgiveness. Jesus says, 'Settle matters quickly with your adversary who is taking you to court. Do it while you are still with him on the way, or he may hand you over to the judge, and the judge may hand you over to the officer, and you may be thrown into prison' (Matthew 5:25). This is not only good practical advice, it is good spiritual advice too.

The second block to joy is linked to the first. Repentance implies *restoration*. Zacchaeus, the little tax collector who climbed a sycamore tree to see Jesus, was overjoyed when Jesus became a guest in his home. Though tax collectors were often cheats in those days, there was no block in the way of Zacchaeus' capacity for joy. Perhaps it was to his own surprise that he found himself saying, 'Look, Lord! Here and now I give half of my possessions to the poor, and if I have cheated anybody out of anything, I will pay back four times the amount' (Luke 19:8). Some restoration policy!

I am reminded of the letter which is supposed to have been sent to the Income Tax authorities by someone who had been less than honest in filling in his tax-returns: 'Dear Sirs, I am sending you £1,000 unpaid tax because I can't sleep at night. If I still can't sleep, I will send another thousand!' After his encounter with Jesus, Zacchaeus would have no such problem!

The third 'R' is just as important as the other two, and we may be some way along the Christian road before we learn it. If you and I are beginning to mature as Christians, we may find it is precisely at this point that God starts to show us those elements in our way of life which are destructive, disobedient or disproportionate, those things which we need to eliminate by an act of *renunciation*.

Often this is a highly unwelcome experience, and we may be tempted to close our minds to it altogether. But if we block out God's challenge to renunciation, we will find we have also blocked out his joy. We will find ourselves in a mental misery-patch – something that life often does to us in order to bring us to our senses.

Think of Jonah sinking in the swirling water (Jonah 2:3) or sulking in the scorching sun (Jonah 4:8). Nothing went right for him and joy was a stranger while he was disobedient to God's command to renounce his prejudices, or while he was merely obedient under duress. Life can be similarly joyless for us if we stop our ears to God's guidance. Yet in our hearts we know that God never asks us to renounce anything which has any value. When we acknowledge this and bring ourselves to hear and obey him, joy will come flooding back into our lives again.

But it is time for a spiritual health warning. Beware of bogus joy! Think of the shining eyes of those who attended the massive Nazi rallies in World War II. Or of bogus religion where pseudo-joy is emotionally engineered; the after-effects of such orgies of emotion can be worse than any alcoholic hangover. It is here that the wisdom of applying Jesus' principle becomes apparent – 'By their fruit you will recognise them' (Matthew 7:20).

For this reason we must have nothing to do with manipulative methods of evangelism. They may be well meant, but they are always inadmissible and may have disastrous consequences. An enthusiastic group of my congregation once spent the greater part of a night at a residential conference pressing one of our young men to make a decision to accept Jesus as Lord and Saviour. They were jubilant when he did so, and could not understand my reservations about the pressure they had applied. Afterwards, he stopped coming to church altogether. He felt violated. In fact he subsequently told me that the experience had made him an atheist!

If we are fortunate enough to experience real Christian joy, how can we channel it to others? Our joy can be infectious, but it is also likely that some may misunderstand, resent or even be repelled by it. We may have to learn to tune in to the feelings of others and to anticipate their response, and we may find that it is probably best not to attempt to communicate joy directly. So often joy is a by-product of the other things we have been focusing on –

forgiveness, kindness, love, and so on: if we concentrate on channelling those, we will probably channel joy too.

Just what is joy? I believe that its essence consists in penetrating to the heart of reality and discovering that there, in spite of the sorrows of life, all is supremely well. The realisation dawns that, by the grace of God in Christ, we can dwell in that reality, not in pain but through our participation in what God is doing and in the peace that only he can bring. Heaven will be the perfect actualisation of this experience, but even now we may be surprised by a taste of the banquet, a glimpse of the glory, surprised by Jesus, surprised by joy.

With all my heart I wish this joy for myself and I wish it for you. But I can tell you how to kill any chances of it stone dead. Take your eyes from the God revealed by Jesus, and fix them instead adoringly on the 'god' who used to be known by the old-fashioned name of 'Mammon' and joy will have no chance. 'Mammon' is a name for material wealth when it is treated as a god. Jesus warns that there is no possibility we can serve both the real God and the money-god (Matthew 6:24); we have to choose which is our true love. By all appearances, if you turn on a television set and watch the national lottery draw, it seems from the ecstatic expressions of the watching crowds that very many of our fellow citizens are being whipped up into that rapturous love of money which is 'a root of all kinds of evil' (1 Timothy 6:10).

Money is not evil in itself. Far from it – money can provide a challenge to the reality of our discipleship, a test of commitment, a source of service. Rightly handled, it can actually be a channel of joy. But how can we handle this dangerous commodity rightly? We will consider some guidelines in the next chapter.

Chapter 11

RECEIVING THE WORLD'S GOODS

CHANNELLING THE WORLD'S

GOODS

'All things come from you, O God, and of your own
    do we give you.
Accept these tokens of our substance and ourselves.'

I would not like to hazard a guess as to the number of occasions on which I have said those words when I have been
offering up the contents of a collection plate at a service in
church.

Some people have found the words of this prayer to be
true for them personally in a startling and literal way. This
is what happens if at any point you find yourself having to
live by faith. They were certainly true for my own family
when, as I mentioned in chapter nine, the costs involved in
the education of our sons proved more than my entire pay
as a vicar.

They would have been true in just the same way when
Bishop Morris Maddocks and his wife Anne, founders of
the Acorn Christian Healing Trust, had to live by faith in the
early months when Morris had resigned as Bishop of Selby

in order to become Advisor to the Archbishops of Canterbury and York in the ministry of Christian healing, a job which carried a title but no pay at all! Like us, they found that when they trusted themselves and their situation to God, they were never left in need.

However, whether you yourself have ever had the experience of living by faith or not, the prayer at the start of this chapter still represents the basic truth about life. If God is the creator of heaven and earth, then all things come from him, however we may have obtained them. We are never owners: we are always stewards. This is an important element in any true Christian perspective. It is true of all our goods. Our home is God's home. Our car is God's car. Our income is God's income.

I can never forget the debt I owe to the family of the Cornish greengrocer who befriended a group of young soldiers, including me, whilst we were undergoing our period of National Service. Sunday after Sunday, their family car would collect two or three of us to take us to their family church for a service and then home for a slap-up lunch. When I had a week's leave, they invited me to spend the whole of it with them. I found their Christianity was irresistibly infectious simply because of the practical love which flowed so naturally from the way in which they put their time, their talents and their possessions in the hand of God.

They embodied the words of S C Lowry's hymn, 'Son of God, eternal Saviour':

Thine the gold and Thine the silver,
Thine the wealth of land and sea,
We but stewards of Thy bounty,
Held in solemn trust for Thee.

This perspective is symbolised in scripture by the practice of tithing – giving ten per cent of our income back to God, as a sign that it all belongs to him in any case.

The prophet Malachi became very concerned when many of his contemporaries gave up tithing. He stressed the rewards and blessings which come to those who tithe: ' "Bring the whole tithe into the storehouse, that there may be food in my house. Test me in this," says the Lord Almighty, "and see if I will not throw open the floodgates of heaven and pour out so much blessing that you will not have room enough for it" ' (Malachi 3:10). Tithing often seems to have that effect.

John and Gillian were always hard up – until they took the tithing plunge. When they began to tithe, and made sure by means of a banker's order that God's portion of their income was paid out before anything else, they found to their amazement they had more than enough. John said to me, 'We just can't understand it. Our bank account used to be empty before the end of each month, but now the money in it never seems to run out.' He glowed as he told me. The feel-good factor in life had obviously increased for him – even the feel-rich factor!

He reminded me of St Paul's words: 'God loves a cheerful giver' (2 Corinthians 9:7). Givers tend to be cheerful people. I am reminded of a happy soul who once said to me, 'Money is round because it's meant to go round.'

By contrast, those who hold on to their money, keeping it safe from both man and God, tend to be miserable. Bishop Michael Baughen once told me that, in travelling around his diocese speaking about Christian stewardship, it is easy to recognise the people who are the mean and those who are the generous – the generous people look so happy, but the mean look so miserable.

The prophet Malachi goes so far as to say that those who

withhold God's tithe are actually robbing God, and to those
who rob God he says, 'You are under a curse – the whole
nation of you' (Malachi 3:8).

Jesus looks beyond tithing and addresses our whole attitude to sharing what we have in his awesome description of
the last judgement in chapter 25 of the Gospel of Matthew.
He pictures the nations gathered for judgement. The people
are separated by him, one from another 'as a shepherd sep-
arates the sheep from the goats', sheep on the right, goats on
the left:

> 'Then the King will say to those on his right, "Come,
> you who are blessed by my Father; take your inheri-
> tance, the kingdom prepared for you since the cre-
> ation of the world. For I was hungry and you gave
> me something to eat, I was thirsty and you gave me
> something to drink, I was a stranger and you invited
> me in, I needed clothes and you clothed me, I was
> sick and you looked after me, I was in prison and
> you came to visit me."
>
> 'Then the righteous will answer him, "Lord,
> when did we see you hungry and feed you, or thirsty
> and give you something to drink? When did we see
> you a stranger and invite you in, or needing clothes
> and clothe you? When did we see you sick or in
> prison and go to visit you?"
>
> 'The King will reply, "I tell you the truth, what-
> ever you did for one of the least of these brothers of
> mine, you did for me."
>
> 'Then he will say to those on his left, "Depart
> from me, you who are cursed, into the eternal fire
> prepared for the devil and his angels. For I was hun-
> gry and you gave me nothing to eat, I was thirsty and
> you gave me nothing to drink, I was a stranger and

you did not invite me in, I needed clothes and you
did not clothe me, I was sick and in prison, and you
did not look after me."

'They also will answer, "Lord, when did we see
you hungry or thirsty or a stranger or needing clothes
or sick or in prison, and did not help you?"

'He will reply, "I tell you the truth, whatever
you did not do for one of the least of these, you did
not do for me."

'Then they will go away to eternal punishment,
but the righteous to eternal life.' *(Matthew 25:34–46)*

Jesus seems to be saying that what we release now in love
and compassion will await us in heaven, whereas what we
hold on to here will remain earthbound. Our possessions will
start to hold on to us, to possess us. They will interfere with
our relationship with Christ, and with our eternal destiny. In
other words, to use the trenchant slogan coined some years
ago by the Church Mission Society, Jesus is saying, 'The
mean are damned'. To illustrate this uncomfortable truth I
should like to indulge in another children's story.

Gilbert lived in a big house. He was a rich man, mainly
because he never gave anything away. When a collector for
overseas aid came along, he set the dog on him. He never
went to church, so he never put anything on the collection
plate. At Christmas he only gave presents to people he
thought would give him better presents back. He ate big
fancy meals, but he never invited anyone to share them
unless they were rich and important.

Sidney lived next door, in a smaller house because he
was not so rich. He gave away a proportion of everything he
earned to the church he went to, and he also gave to a whole
range of charities and good causes. Gilbert thought he was
mad! But though Sidney had only a small house, it always

seemed full of people. He liked having friends around, to share what he had. Gilbert regarded him as a bit of a fool, a soft touch.

One day they both died, and they were taken by an angel to a large house. This house seemed to have many rooms in it. They entered the house, and Gilbert and Sidney were ushered into a room containing a table with a sumptuous feast laid out on it.

Gilbert said, 'This is marvellous! It's just what I fancy.'

But the angel said, 'No, that's for Sidney. But there is a table for you.'

Leaving Sidney to enjoy his feast, the angel took Gilbert into another room. Inside it was a second table, but this one had nothing on it but a dry stale crust and a glass of water.

Gilbert said, 'But this isn't fair!'

The angel replied, 'We do have an excellent chef here; but the rule is that when he is preparing meals he can only use whatever you have given away on earth. Well, once you gave some stale bread to a seagull when you were on holiday. And once you gave a glass of water to a lady who felt faint. So, *this* is your banquet.'

'I don't call this a banquet,' said Gilbert. 'In fact, I don't call this heaven at all – I call it hell!'

The angel said, 'Ah, you've noticed, have you?'

You might be feeling rather uncomfortable and ill at ease by now, but if you are, then congratulations for having got this far! I do understand the discomfort which any serious consideration of Christian stewardship brings: applying the input/output principle can be especially painful in matters of income. I know it from my own experience. When I first brought myself to sign a covenant in favour of my local church, I actually experienced a pain in my hand! My mind knew I was doing the right thing, but my meanness of soul had to find a way of registering its protest.

Sinners like ourselves do not find it easy to begin tithing. Sometimes we have to move towards it by very gradual stages. This is what happened at our PCC. At the time when we took our first tentative steps to becoming a tithing church, we were going through a period of considerable financial stringency and were facing the prospect of a horrendously large deficit.

It was then that Matthew, one of our younger members, said that he believed our troubles were related to the fact that we centred our financial thinking upon our own needs. It was true that we gave away the proceeds of various special efforts, but the money put on the collection plate in church or which came by direct giving was all earmarked for parish use.

Matthew proposed that from this point on, one per cent of our income should be detached from the financial provision for the church and given to those in need outside it. Rather to our own surprise we found ourselves carrying the proposal, and again to our surprise we found that our financial crisis seemed to melt away.

Next year Matthew proposed that the amount given away should increase to two per cent, and the proposal was again carried, as were proposals in subsequent years that we should increase this amount to three per cent and then five per cent and then seven per cent and finally ten per cent.

Now we allocate ten per cent of our income to a separate 'Christian giving' account. It is a real joy to be able to send thousands of pounds to missionary societies and aid societies in and beyond our country. On top of this, we still have special efforts for various good and needy causes. At last as a church we have become a body in which our financial life embodies the biblical principle of giving God both tithes and offerings.

As we have taken this journey into stewardship, we have

always found that the needs of our own church have been met. This seems to be a characteristic of tithe-and-offering living, and in fact Jesus promises as much (Matthew 6:33). Now individual church members are beginning to consider the same journey into stewardship which the church as a whole has made. Of course, some are further along the way than others, and some have hardly started.

Which category do you come into? Are you prepared to take the risk of asking, 'What do you want me to do, Lord, with *your* money?'

Chapter 12

WARNING!

RECEIVING EVIL INFLUENCES

CHANNELLING EVIL INFLUENCES

This is meant to be, in the main, a positive and optimistic book: but everything has its dark side and the input/output principle is no exception.

I read recently of a woman who, after she had contracted AIDS, made it her aim to infect as many men as possible with it. It is well known that abusers of children are often people who were themselves abused in childhood and who, consciously or unconsciously, repeat history. Adolf Hitler had a cruel father and, subsequently, channelled and magnified that cruelty as he exercised power without mercy.

If these seem spectacular, it is not difficult to find more work-a-day examples of the same thing. Think for instance of the phenomenon of displaced anger, of the man who is criticised or humiliated by his boss, but who cannot say anything at the time because he is afraid of losing his job. When he gets home, however, he snaps at his wife, loses his temper with the children and maybe even kicks the cat!

The bad news is that Christians are not immune from this dark side of the input/output principle. We can receive and channel undesirable influences. It was to Peter that Jesus said the terrible words, 'Get behind me, Satan!' (Mark 8:33). If Peter, who was Jesus' dear friend and follower, could become a channel of dark and dangerous forces, you and I can certainly not claim to be immune from them. Where do they come from, these evil influences which we may find ourselves channelling from time to time?

The Book of Common Prayer points to three major sources of evil – the world, the flesh and the devil. In the service of baptism, godparents are required to renounce all three as they promise to exercise responsibility for the well-being of their godchildren. The same teaching appears in these words from the Litany:

> … from all the deceits of the world, the flesh, and the devil,
>> *Good Lord, deliver us.*

And in this rather longer prayer:

> Lord God Almighty,
> Grant your people grace
> to withstand the temptations
> of the world, the flesh and the devil,
> and with pure hearts and minds
> to follow you, the only God:
> through Jesus Christ our Lord,
> Amen.

If we are wise, we will not neglect the spiritual health warning in these words. The world, the flesh and the devil are three sources of trouble which merit serious consideration. It seems sensible to think about them in that order.

• *The world*

God loves this world (John 3:16), but all too often the world does not return God's love: it has become enemy-occupied territory (1 John 5:19) The world's standards are not God's standards. The world's influence on us is not a godly influence. We can all too easily find that what we are receiving from this world we are also channelling back, and that this process is not for our good or for anyone else's.

The child abuser is a good example of this. As I said before, very often he or she is only carrying on the pattern of abuse – it is the only way to relate that they know of. So another innocent victim is created, who in turn may repeat the pattern. Many terrorists, world-wide, can also repeat patterns of violence that they themselves have experienced, the hate in their heart and in their lives a result of the hateful treatment that they and those they love have themselves received. And so a Bosnia is born, or a Rwanda – or a Northern Ireland.

Much bitterness of spirit owes its origin to the injustice and violence of the world. I was helped to understand the bitterness which some Welsh people feel towards the English when an elderly Welsh woman told me how her father had been beaten at school for the offence of speaking Welsh. In his day, only English was permitted. She was struggling – God bless her – not to be a channel of bitterness herself. But it takes a remarkable person to respond with love when you or your family are treated with violence. Archbishop Desmond Tutu has managed to be such a person in South Africa. By the grace of God he has responded to the obscenity of apartheid with cheerfulness and love.

You and I are called by God to do something similar, though probably in much less heroic ways. So how do we cope with the ravages of the world? If we are treated spitefully, do we manage, by the grace of God, not to become channels of spite? If we are treated meanly, does it make us mean people? If we hear malicious gossip, does it end with us or are we tempted to become the channels of malice ourselves?

The God who is Love (1 John 4:8) is able to love this world without being polluted by the world. We certainly need his power and protection if we ourselves are to avoid receiving and channelling the destructive influences in society to our own hurt and the hurt of others.

To make this more difficult, evil influences not only come to us from the outer world, but also from our inner world, from what the Bible calls 'the flesh'.

• *The flesh*
This is the biblical term (eg see 'sinful nature', Romans 8:13) for human nature gone wrong, spoilt by the sinfulness which is so much a part of us. The sin which characterises human nature is of two sorts.

First, there is *inherited* (or original) sin. As the psalmist says of himself, 'Surely I was sinful at birth, sinful from the time my mother conceived me' (Psalm 51:5). If this seems hard, it does accord with the facts of life as we experience it. We do not come into this world with a totally clean sheet. Life's design has already started to be marked out upon us. We can see physical evidence of this: one person will have her father's chin, another his mother's eyes. We can see it in our abilities and talents: for example, I was born with the musical ability that has characterised so many of my mother's family. We can also see mental, emotional and spiritual evidence. We can be grateful for much of our inheritance, but it is flawed because we come from a flawed and sinful species. I remember an elderly clergyman bemoaning the fact he found it almost impossible not to replicate his father's bad temper.

Apart from the sinful tendencies we inherit, there are *additional personal sins* which we choose for ourselves – for example, deliberate dishonesty. The psalmist acknowledges that, along with the sinfulness he inherited at birth, there are plenty of ways in which he had pursued sins of his very own. He confesses to God, 'Against you, you only, have I sinned and done what is evil in your sight' (Psalm 51:4).

This combination of inherited and personal sinfulness means that quite apart from the damage that the world does to us, all too often we do ourselves no good either. We are victims, and sometimes willing victims of 'the flesh'. If we are too willing to co-operate with our sinful tendencies, there comes a point where co-operation is hardly needed. Our sins can become 'besetting sins': they hold us captive.

To this lethal combination of the world and the flesh we must now add a third source of trouble.

• *The devil*

Some people regard the devil as no more than a figurative and picturesque way of describing the force of evil that is discernible in the world and the flesh. But I believe *The Book of Common Prayer* is right to regard the devil as a third, quite separate, source of evil.

Jesus certainly makes this distinction himself and takes the devil literally (eg Luke 22:31). His teaching acknowledges the fact that human beings are not the only intelligent created beings in this universe, nor are we the only created beings to have misused God's gift of freedom and to have fallen away from our Maker. There also exists a mysterious angelic realm, not normally visible to our limited human senses. Satan (or the devil) is a powerful member of this order and is in open rebellion against God. He makes it his aim to wreak havoc within creation, and he has Planet Earth in his sights as a special target.

The good news is that Satan is a created being, with all the limitations that this implies. Unlike God, Satan can only be in one place at a time: we must never attribute omnipresence to him. By contrast, Jesus is *always* with us: this is his final promise (Matthew 28:20). Not so with Satan. When we say 'the devil has tempted me', we flatter ourselves. It is most unlikely that we are important enough to merit his personal attention. Jesus had to meet the devil face to face when he was tempted in the desert (Matthew 4:1–11), and Judas merited his personal attention (John 13:2). But it is improbable in the extreme that you and I will ever do so. Satan has much bigger fish to fry!

However, the bad news is that a host of lesser spirits also defected from God to side with Satan. These evil spirits work with him, under his control, as a sort of Mafia. It is far from impossible that at some point we may experience the malign influence of one of these minions of Satan. This is why we should never trifle with the occult, even apparently harmless things like horoscopes in newspapers!

Of course, we should never assume that there is demonic influence in a situation until we have exhausted all other possibilities. There are mental illnesses which have as a symptom the conviction that demons, or even the devil himself, are at work in the life of the sick person. However, having said this, we cannot ignore the fact that Jesus takes very seriously the possibility that Satan's minions play an active part in human life, and he encourages us to take their involvement seriously too (Luke 11:24–26). C S Lewis' famous book, *The Screwtape Letters* – in which a senior devil instructs a junior devil in the art of tempting – may not be as fanciful as one might think. Indeed, Lewis felt himself under deep oppression while he was writing the book. As Thomas More has said, 'The devil cannot endure to be mocked', and the odds are that his minions do not like it either.

In my own ministry I have dealt with several people whose troubles seemed to come from the satanic realm, and in my previous parish I went through a very strange experience when we decided to take the ministry of Christian healing seriously. It happened simultaneously to all three clergy, the churchwardens and the church secretary. It was a horrible thing, full of morbid fancies and the temptation to despair. Previously I had assumed that only the attractive could tempt, but it is not so. Strangely enough, my own experience of this oppression took place actually during a holiday period. All around me were scenes of beauty, and there were plenty of opportunities for leisure and enjoyment. Yet through it all there was something horrid, hard to describe, a sort of weight of darkness, pressing down. It was a relief to find that others were going through it too. With mutual support and prayer it passed. It has been suggested to us that we were under some sort of attack, and certainly this is just what it felt like.

Now that we have identified the world, the flesh and the devil as sources of evil influence, where do we go from here? How can we guard against receiving these influences and channelling them to others?

In fact, how can we do more than be on guard? How can we go on the offensive as soldiers of Jesus Christ?

Chapter 13

ONWARD, CHRISTIAN SOLDIERS

Before my ordination I spent two years in the army as a National Serviceman. There my fellow conscripts and I learned the importance of the company orders which were posted daily outside the orderly room setting out our duties for that day. This chapter is an attempt to suggest some 'company-orders' for Christian soldiers, a mini-manual for those engaged in basic training for spiritual warfare. I do hope it may go some way towards helping you deal with any evil influences that may come your way.

It is important to take evil seriously – but not too seriously. In his preface to *The Screwtape Letters,* C S Lewis writes: 'There are two equal and opposite errors which our race can fall into about the devils. One is to disbelieve in their existence. The other is to believe and to feel an excessive and unhealthy interest in them.' The same could be said about evil as a whole.

We present no danger to evil if we *pretend* it does not exist. In the words of the Roman poet Virgil, 'Sin fattens and flourishes when kept secret'. On the other hand, if we do become aware of the existence of evil, the devil likes it best if we are paralysed by that awareness. He likes us to be overwhelmed with depression and despair. He presents himself as irresistible. But remember what Jesus had to say of the devil: 'He is a liar and the father of lies' (John 8:44).

The way to keep a sense of *perspective* is to see that, though we take evil seriously, we take God and goodness *more* seriously. I love the story of the old man who used to claim he would be saved by his good looks. When he was asked about this, he would explain that he was referring to the 'good looks' he had at Jesus. In the words of Hebrews, 'Let us fix our eyes on Jesus, the author and perfecter of our faith' (Hebrews 12:2).

With a sense of perspective will come *protection*. There is no better guidance to Christian protection than the mighty words about the armour of God in Ephesians:

Put on the full armour of God so that you can take your stand against the devil's schemes. For our strug-gle is not against flesh and blood, but against the rulers, against the authorities, against the powers of this dark world and against the spiritual forces of evil in the heavenly realms. Therefore put on the full armour of God so that when the day of evil comes, you may be able to stand your ground, and after you have done everything, to stand. Stand firm then, with the belt of truth buckled round your waist, with the breastplate of righteousness in place, and with your feet fitted with the readiness that comes from the gospel of peace. In addition to all this, take up the shield of faith, with which you can extinguish all the flaming arrows of the evil one. Take the helmet of salvation and the sword of the Spirit, which is the word of God. *(Ephesians 6:13–17)*

You may like to use this passage as a check-list to ensure that you have the right personal protection in place.

However, just in case our protection level is inadequate and something nasty has somehow slipped in and taken hold, it is good to know that the power of God available to us is more than sufficient to deal with any situation. All we have to do is to ask for deliverance in the name of Jesus. It is usually adequate to do this quietly and privately during our personal prayer time. There is a method of prayer which provides for this need should it arise. It is a way of practising the presence of the risen Christ.

First, we claim the scriptural promise of his presence (Matthew 28:20). Then we acknowledge and receive his love. We picture Christ's healing hands upon us and open ourselves to his exorcising power. If there is any sin, any negativity, any evil or alien element in us, we expose it to his rebuke and allow him to cast it out, knowing that the forces of evil must retreat before him unless we give them sanctuary.

There is even a mini-exorcism at the heart of the Lord's Prayer. Jesus commands us to pray, 'Deliver us from evil'. If we do so and mean it, we can and should expect that prayer to be answered.

However, if the evil influence has its claws hooked deeply into our soul, we may need some help from our fellow Christians. We should never be ashamed to ask for this help. The church is not a club for saints, but a hospital for sinners. 'Spiritual operations' are meant to be a feature of the church's 'hospital life'. Your clergy or church leaders should be able to help, or at least they should know where help is on offer.

It is important to be aware of the danger of inner emptiness. Listen to these words of Jesus:

'When an evil spirit comes out of a man, it goes through arid places seeking rest and does not find it. Then it says, "I will return to the house I left." When it arrives it finds the house swept clean and put in order. Then it goes and takes seven other spirits more wicked than itself, and they go in and live there. And the final condition of that man is worse than the first.' *(Luke 11:24–26)*

Because of this, it is never enough to cast out the undesirable things. They must be replaced by that which is positively desirable. This will involve positive thinking: 'whatever is true, whatever is noble, whatever is right, whatever is pure, whatever is admirable – if anything is excellent or praiseworthy – think about such things' (Philippians 4:8).

It involves positive invitation. We need to be filled with all that is best, and Jesus *is* all that is best. He is everything in St Paul's list – true, noble, right, pure, admirable, excellent and praiseworthy. And Jesus is ours for the asking.

I am told that Archbishop William Temple's favourite prayer was this:

Into my heart,
Into my heart,
Into my heart, Lord Jesus,
Come in today,
Come in to stay,
Come into my heart, Lord Jesus.

It is our privilege to pray this prayer, or something like it, at the beginning of our Christian journey, and then to reaffirm it day by day, more and more deeply, more and more completely – rejoicing as we do so that Jesus is the Saviour who likes to say 'Yes.' We should expect Christ's presence (Revelation 3:20).

We should also expect Christ's victory, for he means us to share it. Note that the Roman soldier's armour – which forms the basis for St Paul's words in Ephesians 6:11–17 –gives protection only when he is advancing. St Paul is telling us that we too are to be armed for attack. It is surprising how often our mental picture is precisely the opposite. We even manage to misinterpret Sabine Baring Gould's marvellous hymn, 'Onward, Christian soldiers'. We tend to suppose that the line 'Gates of hell can never 'gainst the church prevail' means that we will be protected if the forces of hell attack us. In fact, if we think about it, the picture language is that of hell being like a city under siege by the armies of Christ's church. Hell's gates are strong, but they are not strong enough. We are armed for the attack, and Christ himself is leading us. In the long run, hell has no chance; its foundations are already crumbling.

Let's enjoy a couple of verses from Goulding's hymn which is based on the King James Version of Matthew 16:18: they should help to dispel any negative feelings that may be lingering from the last chapter.

Onward, Christian soldiers,
Marching as to war,
With the cross of Jesus
Going on before!
Christ, the royal Master,
Leads against the foe;
Forward into battle,
See, his banners go!

Onward, Christian soldiers!
Marching as to war,
With the cross of Jesus
Going on before.

At the sign of triumph
Satan's host doth flee;
On then, Christian soldiers,
On to victory!
Hell's foundations quiver
At the shout of praise;
Brothers, lift your voices;
Loud your anthems raise:

Onward, Christian soldiers!
Marching as to war,
With the cross of Jesus
Going on before. •

If God is God, then those whose will it is to stand for God must be on the winning side. The enemies of God cannot be on the winning side.

The Bible hammers this home. Jesus himself hammers this home. In the words of 'Onward, Christian soldiers', 'We have Christ's own promise and that cannot fail'.

When Jesus sent seventy-two of his followers out on a mission of teaching and healing, he equipped them for spiritual warfare, and they conquered in his name. They reported back to him, 'Lord, even the demons submit to us in your name.' And his reply? 'I saw Satan fall like lightning from heaven' (Luke 10:17–18). Our equipment is even better than that of the disciples. They went out *for* him: we are invited to go out *with* him.

Ultimately, the world and the flesh will be purged and reclaimed for God. As for the serried ranks of the hosts of darkness, they have no hope. Eternal fire awaits them, 'prepared for the devil and his angels' (Matthew 25:41). So in the words of James 4:7, 'Resist the devil and he will flee from you.'

We have seen that at one point St Peter became Satan's mouthpiece incurring that terrible rebuke from Jesus (Mark 8:33). Peter could have slunk away from his Christian calling in confusion and self-contempt. But Jesus permitted no such course (Luke 22:31). He gave Peter time to balance the fact that he was a sinner, capable of both receiving and channelling evil influences, with the fact that, in spite of his sinful nature, God is mighty and was calling him both to service and to glory in Christ. When he fully understood the implications of this, Peter had this piece of measured advice for his fellow Christians and for us:

Humble yourselves, therefore, under God's mighty hand, that he may lift you up in due time. Cast all your anxiety on him because he cares for you.

Be self-controlled and alert. Your enemy the devil prowls around like a roaring lion looking for someone to devour. Resist him, standing firm in the faith, because you know that your brothers throughout the world are undergoing the same kind of sufferings.

And the God of all grace, who called you to his eternal glory in Christ, after you have suffered a little while, will himself restore you and make you strong, firm and steadfast. To him be the power for ever and ever. Amen. *(1 Peter 5:6–11)*

Chapter 14

RECEIVING JESUS

CHANNELLING JESUS

We come now to the very heart of the message of this book.

Christians believe that the way to receive and channel forgiveness, love, hope, joy, and all the other good things discussed so far – and, conversely, the way neither to receive nor channel the evil influences we may experience – is quite simply to receive and to channel Jesus himself.

The New Testament says that the heart of Christian living is to be *en Christo* which literally means 'in Christ'. According to the German scholar, Adolf Deissmann, St Paul uses these words or their equivalent 164 times. I like the translation of these words in the *Good News* Bible as 'union with Christ.'

Union with Christ is a life-transforming experience. St Paul says that it involves nothing less than 'new creation' (2 Corinthians 5:17). When I preach, I find myself continually using the phrase, 'Jesus makes a difference'. One of my former colleagues used to say that we should have the words etched in the stonework above the church door. But I would much prefer them to be etched in the heart of every one of

our church members. To put the same thought in the termi-
nology of this book, Jesus himself is the essence of
Christian input, and the difference he makes is the essence
of Christian output.

Jesus is never a non-event. He is '*the* way (John 14:6) –
the Father's way through to us, and our way through to the
Father. He is also the supreme activator of the Holy Spirit.
Jesus never works upon or within us in isolation from the
Father and the Spirit, because God the Father, God the Son
and God the Holy Spirit are one God. Jesus is our Father's
greatest gift to us and, as we receive the Son from the
Father, the Spirit moves in us. The Holy Spirit is involved
in the process of our receiving Jesus and channelling Jesus.

However, though we are called to do our level best as
Christians, we are not called to *depend* upon our level best:
'Our competence comes from God' (2 Corinthians 3:5).

I cannot resist telling you a final children's story which
the younger members of my church have enjoyed. It is
based loosely on part of a fairly well-known story, that of
'The Brave Little Tailor', but I have developed it into a
parable that can speak both to children and adults alike.

Once upon a time there was a village which was ter-
rorised by a big and bad-tempered giant. He bullied everybody and made them very unhappy. He took whatever he
wanted – beef from the butcher, bread from the baker, beer
from the brewer and he never paid anybody for anything. If
anyone complained, they would find their windows would
be smashed and their flower-beds trampled down. The giant
particularly liked to harass and humiliate those who were
small and defenceless, and one of his special victims was a
little tailor, a cheerful man who was good at his job, kind to
his neighbours and loved by everyone – except the giant.
For some reason the little tailor's friendly smile infuriated
the giant. When he met him, he would curse him soundly,

and sometimes he would push him over and kick dust in his face.

But one market day everyone had a great surprise. The giant was being his usual horrible self, taking what he liked, kicking over the stall of anyone who objected, terrifying the dogs and cats, and making the children cry. Then into the centre of the market square walked the little tailor and, to everybody's amazement, he issued a challenge to the giant.

Each was to select something of his choice and throw it into the air. Whoever achieved the greater height would be the winner. 'If you win,' said the little tailor, 'I will be your slave for ever. If I win, you shall obey me, and I will give you just one order – to leave this village and never return.'

The giant was jubilant. He looked at his own powerful arm muscles and was sure he would win – and he certainly fancied having the tailor as his personal slave. He selected a heavy rock and with a mighty heave threw it high into the air – higher than the houses, higher than the church spire – till finally it fell to earth, completely smashing the village telephone kiosk as it did so .

But then the little tailor lifted something in his hands and released it into the air. Up and up it went, higher and higher, till it was out of sight. It was a dove. And so, against all the odds, the little tailor was the victor and the giant skulked away.

The little tailor provides a pattern for Christian living not only by his manner of life but also by his methodology. Christian living is not a matter of hoisting and heaving like the giant with his hunk of rock. The Christian takes into his hands that which has beauty and momentum in its own right – Jesus' gift to us when we accept union with him, which is not the dead weight of duty but the living gift of the Holy Spirit, often symbolised by a soaring dove (eg Matthew 3:16).

Jesus is both the supreme gift-bringer and the supreme gift. It is true that we are called to service, but first we are called to rest and rejoice in his presence, receiving all that he brings to us in his pierced hands and his generous heart.

My wife, Eira, in a booklet she is currently preparing in conjunction with a Christian relaxation tape, says we are invited to be 'Son-bathers', soaking up the Son, glowing with the Son's warmth and light. It is a biblical image. When the prophet Malachi predicts the coming of the Messiah (Malachi 4:2), he describes him as the 'sun of righteousness' and says that his healing input will enable us to have a notable output: 'You will go out and leap', equipped with God's freedom for God's fight.

It is an essential part of Christian output to lead others out of this world's darkness towards God's shining Son. We can offer no greater gift to another human being than the gift of Jesus. In the ringing words which conclude the letter of St James, 'My brothers, if one of you should wander from the truth, and someone should bring him back, remember this; whoever turns a sinner from the error of his ways will save him from death and cover over a multitude of sins'. Just as receiving Jesus is a matter of life and death, so channelling Jesus is also a matter of life and death.

How are we to be channels of the Son of God to others? There are three ways. We are to be mirrors, speakers, and lovers.

As mirrors we are to reflect something – however little – of the reality of Jesus' nature. When Malcolm, our local Methodist minister, recently left our neighbourhood to work in a new area, many tributes were made to his ministry at his farewell party. But I am sure that the one he will treasure most came from a woman who said very simply that what she had most valued in him was that he had helped her to know Jesus, because she had seen so much of Jesus in him.

I had often thought the same thing. When I looked at Malcolm, I saw Jesus again and again. There could be no higher tribute. To some extent it should be possible to say this of every Christian.

Second, we are called to be the Saviour's speakers, prepared to communicate in words, however hesitantly, what Jesus means to us. In spite of the fact that this book is packed with references from scripture, and rightly so, the ordinary Christian does not need to bombard people with scripture texts. All we need is to be prepared to speak – however fumbling our form of words may be – of just how much it means to us to take Jesus Christ seriously and to know that he takes us seriously too. There may be one person at this moment who will not hear of the relevance of the Christian faith unless he or she hears it from *you*!

So we are called, you and I, to be mirrors and speakers. But this may be to no avail unless we are also lovers. I shall never forget seeing a truculent little boy sitting on a brick wall outside a church hall where he had just been to Sunday School. When I asked him what was wrong, he named his Sunday School teacher and said, 'You can't tell me *he* loves me!' His Sunday School teacher was, in fact, quite an eloquent man, but as St Paul said in 1 Corinthians 13:1, 'If I speak in the tongues of men and of angels, but have not love, I am only a resounding gong or a clanging cymbal.'

Just think. If, by the grace of God and the input and output of the living Christ, you and I manage in some way, however small, to be his mirrors, his speakers, his lovers, then we will channel the very best this world can hold.

In fact the best is to be found beyond this world. So read on.

Chapter 15

RECEIVING ETERNAL LIFE

CHANNELLING ETERNAL LIFE

'God so loved the world that he gave his one and
only Son, that whoever believes in him shall not per-
ish but have eternal life.' (John 3:16.)

In this last chapter, it will be our presumptuous purpose to
lift the curtain of eternity for a moment. If God is infinite,
then Christian input and output must reflect something of
his infinity. Jesus tells his followers that we are to receive
the gift of eternal life from his saving hands and heart: 'I am
the resurrection and the life. He who believes in me will
live, even though he dies' (John 11:25). Furthermore, we
are to pass this gift of eternal life on to others. We are to be
channels as well as receivers. As we saw in chapter 13, we
are called so to communicate Jesus to our neighbour that, in
the words of St James, the result is to 'save him from death
and cover over a multitude of sins' (James 5:20).

Of course, comprehending eternal life is totally beyond
us here and now – beyond our tiny minds, beyond our limited vocabulary: 'No eye has seen, no ear heard, no mind

has conceived what God has prepared for those who love him' (1 Corinthians 2:9).

A few intrepid souls have taken the risk of trying to express the inexpressible. One of C S Lewis' finest (and perhaps most undervalued) books is a fantasy story called *The Great Divorce*, an account of a coach trip from hell to heaven. In the book C S Lewis imagines himself being given a tour of heaven by George Macdonald whom, for much of his life, he regarded as a mentor and guide in spiritual matters. One of the citizens of eternity they encounter is a shining Lady, a sort of heavenly queen, full of beauty and joy and life:

> 'Is it …? Is it …?' asked Lewis.
> 'Not at all,' said Macdonald, 'it's someone ye'll never have heard of. Her name on earth was Sarah Smith and she lived at Golders Green'.
> 'She seems to be … well, a person of particular importance?'
> 'Aye, she is one of the great ones.'
> 'And who are all these …?'
> 'They are her sons and daughters … In her they became themselves. And now the abundance of life she has in Christ from the Father flows over into them.'

I have for years found myself fascinated by Sarah Smith. She is portrayed as such a receiver and such a channel of eternal life. It is tantalising that C S Lewis gives us so few hints about the person she was on earth, and I have found myself wondering what kind of life she might have led in Golders Green to end in such glorious eternal fruition. My imagination has worked upon her and, if I may, I would like to share the result. C S Lewis would have done better but, in his absence, Sarah Smith – this is your life!

Sarah was an ordinary person – very ordinary. Her parents used to joke that when wealth, brains and beauty were given out, she was in the wrong queue.

They were distinctly relieved when a man came along who was prepared to marry her, but in truth it was not much of a marriage. Frank Smith, her husband, soon let it be known that she was not much of a catch. He liked the comfortable home she provided, but took it all for granted. When they were not able to have children, he made no secret that he thought it was all her fault. He was not impressed when she took a job as a cleaner in a large office block nearby. Very early in the morning she would creep out of the house and clean the offices. She was a good cleaner and made everything sparkle. Even the managing director noticed, but it was a long time before he bothered to find out who was responsible.

Sarah was often late getting home. She had a little kitchen in the small room where she kept her cleaning equipment, and she was allowed to make herself a cup of tea or coffee before she left. She was quite surprised that, month by month, more and more of the office workers seemed to drop in and scrounge a cup of coffee off her as they arrived for work.

In fact, she did have a gift – an important one. People wanted to talk to her, especially people who were finding life difficult. It was a bit like the wounded birds she found in the garden or the stray dogs who came to the door. She could not resist caring for them, and it was the same with wounded human beings. The managing director used to boast that his firm seemed not to need a welfare officer. The truth was that increasingly Sarah became the welfare officer.

Of course, she did not get paid for it. 'She's a fool to herself,' said her husband.

It was much the same in the little chapel Sarah went to on a Sunday. She never achieved a position of leadership. Her place was in the kitchen, brewing and serving the tea and washing the teacups afterwards. Yet it was probably true that more people poured out their hearts in Sarah's kitchen than in the minister's study.

She outlived her husband and, because she found she had spare time, she took an extra job as a tea-time lollipop lady, showing children across the busy road outside a local school. It was not long before lots of them came to think of her as an unofficial granny.

She was certainly needed. The traffic was terrible. Her traffic-crossing was an accident waiting to happen – and one day it did. She and six children were in the middle of the road when a juggernaut lorry went out of control and came screaming towards them.

She managed to push the children out of the way, but could do nothing to save her own life. Her frail body was tossed into the air as the juggernaut hit her. Sarah Smith herself never came down again.

She would have been amazed at her funeral. The little chapel was packed. Even the managing director was there. People who could not find space in the building had to stand on the pavement outside. But for Sarah herself there was an even greater surprise in store.

As she opened her eyes the light was dazzling, and yet she felt at home as never before. The most wonderful pair of eyes she had ever seen were looking deeply, lovingly into her.

She heard herself say, 'It's You, isn't it?'

Jesus replied, 'Of course it is,' and put his arms around her.

It was then that she became aware of the others – hundreds of them, all around, all looking at her with inexpressible joy.

She seemed to know them but couldn't be sure. 'Who are these, Lord?' she asked.

Jesus smiled: 'This is your welcoming committee, Sarah. These are your Friends, your Followers, your Family in Heaven. It will be their joy to attend you and acknowledge you for ever.'

'There must be some mistake, Lord,' said Sarah. 'I only cleaned rooms and served tea.'

'It's more than rooms you've cleaned, my Love,' said Jesus. 'You feel at home because you've been in heaven for years – or rather, heaven has been in you. And it's been spilling out from you.

'You weren't just serving tea, you know. You were serving the water of life, the wine of heaven. You were serving *me*.'

Some distance away a man called Lewis was walking with another called Macdonald.

(And so, to go back to the words of *The Great Divorce*...)

'Is it ...? Is it ...?' asked Lewis.

'Not at all' said Macdonald, 'it's someone ye'll never have heard of. Her name on earth was Sarah Smith and she lived at Golders Green.'

'She seems to be ... well, a person of particular importance?'

'Aye, she is one of the great ones.'

'And who are all these...?'

'They are her sons and daughters ... In her they became themselves. And now the abundance of life she has in Christ from the Father flows over into them.'

Jesus said, 'Whoever believes in me ... streams of living water will flow from within him' (John 7:38). You do not have to be rich, powerful, famous, strong in body or brilliant in mind to have eternal life welling in you and flowing from you. An epitaph of a little disabled priest comes to mind, carved on a gravestone in a country churchyard:

Beneath this yew
A little simple singing priest is laid.
He lived his life,
Of death he was not afraid,
And loved his Maker, though so strangely made.

It sounds as if he might well have been a source of living water to his people. He seems to have been at ease with life and death, and at ease with the Lord. Being at home with the Lord is the essence of eternal life. I love this prayer of William of Thiery:

Lord, I am a countryman,
    coming from my country to yours,
Teach me the laws of your country,
      its way of life,
      its spirit,
So that I may feel at home there.

There is so much we do not and cannot know about heaven. What we do know is that it will be the perfect consummation of our union with Christ:

Dear friends, now we are children of God, and what we will be has not yet been made known. But we know that when he appears, we shall be like him. (1 John 3:2.)

We live in union with the true God, in union with his Son Jesus Christ. This is the true God, and this is eternal life. (1 John 5:20, *Good News Bible*.)

Amazingly, we are called, you and I, to begin to explore eternal life and to do it here and now:

> I write these things to you who believe in the name
> of the Son of God that you may know that you have
> eternal life. (1 John 5:13.)

This is knowledge indeed, and yet it is beyond what we normally mean by knowledge: it is a mystery to cherish and treasure – and to share, unless we are the most selfish and heartless of beings. This has to be the ultimate example of the Christian input/output principle which has been our theme throughout this book.

We started by sitting in my study with Susanna, grieving over her sense of failure and maybe over our own, but now we find ourselves at the base of the foothills of heaven, straining the eyes of our spirit towards an unspeakable beauty. I have found it quite some journey. Words came fairly easily at the start, as we looked together at the negativities of our limited and flawed lives here on earth. But when we scan the horizon of heaven, with each glimpse there comes a silencing of speech, an overwhelming awe too great for words.

So what more is there to be said? Well, perhaps just one thing...

EPILOGUE

THIS IS YOUR LIFE

There is an old legend that after Jesus ended his earthly ministry and returned to heaven, a group of angels gathered round him, wanting to know what he had done and how he had fared.

In answer to their questions, Jesus said, 'I lived on earth as a baby, as a boy and as a man. I taught and healed and loved. I died upon a cross for the sins of the world, and then I rose from the dead and returned to be with you in heaven.'

'But what provision did you make, Lord,' they asked, 'for your continuing ministry?'

'I chose twelve followers to be my apostles. They will form my church and work for my kingdom,' said Jesus.

'But, Lord,' said the angels, 'suppose they fail you. What other plans do you have?'

Jesus replied, 'I have no other plans.'

This is only a legend, an exercise of the imagination, and there seems no harm in letting the imagination process run on. So then …

Seeing the interest of the angels, Jesus decided to

continue meeting with them from time to time to report on developments on Planet Earth.

One day, as they met and discussed the nations of the earth, many mighty concerns were raised.

After the conversation had ranged around various important topics, the smallest angel present plucked up courage and spoke.

'Lord, there is a small corner of earth which you have not mentioned. I visit it from time to time.'

'I know,' said Jesus, 'I watch you go.'

'Though it is small,' said the little angel, 'there seem so many problems there, so many hurts, so much sin.'

'I know that too,' said Jesus, 'but I have a chosen one there.'

'Who can this be?' asked the little angel,

And Jesus answered, '...'

(Stop here and write your own name in the space – do it now or this book will be incomplete!)

'But, Lord,' said the smallest angel, 'can that be a wise choice? I know this human to be unreliable – selfish, wilful, very capable of letting you down.'

'It has always been so with my chosen ones,' replied Jesus.

'Well then,' the smallest angel continued, growing bold, 'suppose they fail you? Have you still no other plan?'

'I have no other plan,' said Jesus. 'But I am their strength and vision. They are my channels, and each is unique, able to do and to be what no other can achieve.'

'But this one seems so frail, so fallible. What will happen next, Lord? What will happen next?' The smallest angel's anguish was almost human as he waited for an answer...

Here I must leave my tale unfinished: the answer to the angel's question must be yours and only yours to give. For this is *your* life and the story is for you to complete as you walk into God's future, remembering always that you will never walk alone.